Isle of the Blest

Isle of the Blest

Jerome Kiely

Mercier Press

Mercier Press

PO Box 5, 5 French Church Street, Cork
24 Lower Abbey Street, Dublin 1

ISBN 1 85635 049 5

A CIP record for this book is available from the British Library.

To
three of the best storytellers
in my life
Sister Augustine Shine in Carlow,
Kate O'Sullivan of Goleen,
and
John Murphy of Skibbereen
this book
is affectionately dedicated

Printed in Ireland by Colour Books Ltd.

Contents

From Ara the holy he sailed to the west,
For though Ara was holy, Hy Brasil was blest.

Gerald Griffin

1

Bishop's Orders

WHEN I FIRST WENT to Maynooth, Inish Capaill to me was only a nail-paring that I had dropped into the Atlantic more than once during geography classes in school when the teacher would get us to sketch a freehand map of Ireland, but, as the years went by, the grotesque little doodle faded off the map, and in its place there rose an island, seven miles by three, with a northern coastline like a group of massive handball alleys, bare and inhospitable, fine pastures sloping to the south, and a harbour shaped like a snowman, the head of it sitting round, squat and neckless on the bigger, squarer trunk.

During the Maynooth years I heard a great deal about it because whenever we pattered about where we might be sent after our ordination, Inish Capaill rose up in our calculations like Hy Brasil, misty, threatening and above all expectant. This was particularly the case when the speculation turned on the five students for Tirella diocese in my class, because it was regarded as inevitable that one of us five would be sent there. For this reason: ever since our bishop had put on the mitre of Tirella he had sent a new administrator to Inish Capaill once every seven years, so if it happened that the new priest was packing his cases for the island in the autumn when you were packing yours as a freshman for Maynooth, you knew that he wouldn't be making his last rattly rounds of the island on his bike until the year when you would be looking at the embarrassed episcopal canvases on the walls of Maynooth for the last time. It so happened that the five of us had put our hold-alls in the luggage van of the train to Maynooth in the year when Fr Blake had put his under a piece of sail-cloth on the boat to Inish Capaill, so it was regarded as a sure thing that one of us would ride the Horse, as we frivolously called it (the Irish name means 'Island of the Horse'). The big question was who would be the jockey.

None of the other four wanted the mount; indeed none of the other thirty Tirella students would so much as look at it from the mainland through a pair of binoculars lest the bishop hear they were at the fence and reckon they wanted to get into the paddock!

An island was all very well, they felt, in the days of saints like Colman and Festin who lived a busy intellectual life in their cells far from the sounds of men and markets, but in our times, with their emphasis on doing not on thinking, a priest on a depopulated island would be condemned to live the life of a drone. I'm not saying our discussions about it were always at that apostolic level; quite the contrary indeed. The four and I were often grinningly told to free-wheel on the theology but to accelerate on the physiology – a very minor subsidiary subject – because as there was no doctor on the island we would find ourselves counting gallstones, cementing fractured hips and slicing open boys' fingers to unhitch fishhooks. And the story was often repeated that the first question the bishop asked when he interviewed his new appointee to Inish Capaill was 'Tell me, Father, are you able to deliver a baby?'

These jokes, however, had more than banter in them: they were rather like the small-scale drawings of bison and mammoth that primitive man sketched on the walls of Lascaux and Niaux to muscle up his own courage: they indicated disquiet with regard to the rearing wild horse out in the Atlantic. How could a man, they asked, not go a trifle crazy at the start of his third week of being marooned in a winter of gales when every book in the house was drained of its last sedative words, and there were only three cigarettes left in the last packet of Players?

Worst of all, they warned, would be the monotony: the monotony of asking the same women about the unchanging health of their indestructible mothers-in-law, the monotony of telling the same altar boy week after week not to leave lumps of the bóithrín all over the sanctuary floor, the monotony of the weather and the talk about the weather, and the monotony of a depressed self.

The cynics used to say you were sentenced to this Alcatraz if you committed a disproportionate number of Maynooth's seven deadly sins: irregularities such as eating chocolate, smuggling newspapers or entering another student's room. This charge I refused absolutely to believe: I could no more admit vindictiveness in a bishop than I could admit injustice in a judge. Besides, it seemed to me that it was in the bishop's own interest to have his priests contented rather than resentful – happiness is a throttle, unhappiness a brake – a state of things which in my view scratched the other four jockeys from the race and left me as the only starter in the Inish Capaill stakes. It was axiomatic in Maynooth that a bishop knew everything about every one of his students. The dean of the college, the parish priest of the student's home parish and interfering old maids from everywhere were held jointly responsible. I therefore took it for granted that he would know I was mad about the sea. As a boy I got more than one box on the ear from the harbour-master of the coastal town where I was born for ducking into his office to find out the launching year and the tonnage of the British and French trawlers which used to fill our harbour with masts and dreams during a bad spell of weather.

But when Bishop Murtagh summoned me to his house a few weeks after I was ordained, he never said a word about midwifery. He had no torn chocolate wrappers or yellowing daily newspapers by courtesy of the Maynooth authorities on display to accuse me of my undisciplined past. There was no reference even to the sea: for all he said, I might have been born in the desert and I might as well be travelling to the island over a causeway. What he did say was: 'Fr Kiely – I shall be appointing you as administrator of Inish Capaill. I shall send you a letter of appointment setting out the date in due course. I shall so arrange it that you will spend a few days with Fr Blake on the island before he leaves for his next assignment. He will explain to you, better than I can, what your various duties will be. I hope you will be very happy there. God bless you and give you every success.'

He said nothing about a seven years' stay. However, as I

walked down his avenue I couldn't help recalling to my mind one of the few passages of the Old Testament that I knew really well, the section where Jacob worked for a period of seven years for Laban while he was betrothed to Laban's daughter. Whether I would find the time, as he did, only like a few days because of the greatness of his love for her, only time, those seven years, would tell.

2

Introductions

THE LETTER ARRIVED. The day came. It was a Friday. I went to Killeggan to board the thirty-foot mail-boat, the *Sapphire* which would bring me out to Inish Capaill for the first time.

On the quay at Killeggan I met Kathy O'Hally who owned the Harbour View pub. What she said made me apprehensive about the welcome that awaited me.

'They are crying bucketfuls out there for Fr Blake,' she said, 'ever since they heard he was leaving.' But what she did reassured me: she steered me into the pub and she gave me a long pliant parcel. 'That's your first dinner on Capaill,' she said. 'Fr Blake rang me up and told me that even if all the bailiffs in Connemara were watching the river, I had to have a salmon going out with you today. And there it is.'

I took the parcel and when I turned around I saw three men seated at a table near the window which gave the pub its harbour viewing name. Each of the three of them had his hands coiled around a pint, and they were looking down at their glasses with the intent gaze of people who might be scanning a compass or scrutinising an experiment in a lab.

'Three of your most pious parishioners, Father,' quipped Kathy. 'And as you'll notice, all staunch Pioneers! Paddy Mallon, skipper of the *Sapphire:* John McHale; Peter Lenny.'

An hour later, Miley O'Shea the boatman brought along the mail-bag and Paddy abandoned the seat in the pub for the stern of his boat, and we cast off for Inish Capaill. There were nine of us aboard: Paddy, Miley, an island woman with two silent children, an Englishwoman with a donkey-load of declamatory camera equipment, John and Peter returning from 'business in Galway' which could mean anything from buying a pair of shoes to selling half a mountain, and my uncertain self.

11

We went by engine and sail, the engine to propel the boat and the sail to steady her and in just about the time that it took the big hand of my watch to do a complete circle we were bearing down on the white beacon at the entrance to Capaill harbour. The *Sapphire* shimmied around the beacon and there in front of me was the neatest and safest haven in all the islands of the west. The water was as shining and smooth as a well-kept kitchen floor, and all around were hills like dressers containing cottages and sheds and a shop and a family hotel and a castle and a church and the priest's house. I can't honestly say whether I saw the castle before the church or the church before the castle or the house before either of them, but before the day was out I had been awarded three firsts in this competition on the principle that dishonesty is the best policy!

The sails were furled. Miley went below. The drumming of the engine took on a slower, less aggressive beat. Paddy brought the *Sapphire* around a generous curve of his own making and put us on a course that would bring us within a seal's whisker of a punt. John went forward with a boat hook and leaned over the bow like a gillie. The big boat bore down on the little one like a rhino charging a gazelle and the gazelle was too frightened to move. Then Miley cut out the engine and the mail-boat made a sound through the water that was all of it boat and none of it machinery. Her hip met the punt's shoulder with a very slight thud. John picked up a long greasy eel of a mooring rope, and the boat shuddered like a lassoed thing and stopped.

To reverse the usual complimentary phrase, mooring the *Sapphire* took a lot longer than it takes to tell. On later trips, when the houses and the harbour had become part of my daily life, I used to read my breviary sitting on the deck during the delay between picking up the moorings and getting into the punt, but on that first day I could see only one kind of hill in front of me and it wasn't the psalmic one of prayer or patience. Especially not the latter. As the minutes slipped away with the cables I felt the impatience of a child outside a toy-shop window: seeing is not enough, one must handle also. I wanted to test if that road was real, if that hill was

12

high, if that church was prayable in and if that bungalow was mine. It was a half an hour if it was a minute before Paddy and the others had satisfied themselves that the *Sapphire* wouldn't go skipper-less to sea. That brought us to punt time.

Paddy and Miley got aboard. Miley began to bail out the punt with the grand gestures of a bishop blessing something big like a factory, and Paddy loaded parcels and suitcases on to the thwarts and boards that weren't yet wet with those ministrations. Cameras, mail-bag and salmon came last in the procession of objects because the last aboard would be first on shore; then we all got into the punt. The children were handed down like parcels and the women were taken down like children who would be sitting on a wall.

I was given an object lesson on how to get into a small boat, followed it successfully and found myself headed for a seat that predestined me to a wet tail. Ah well, I said to myself, like the scrambled eggs and the broken shells, you can't have an island parish without a wet trousers.

Peter Lenny took an oar, gave the *Sapphire* a nasty jab in the stomach with it and pushed us away at last on the course that followed my heart. There was a rowlock opposite the thwart that I was sitting on and I made an attempt to lower an oar into it like a cannon into its carriage but before I had it levelled Miley gently took the dangerous thing out of my hands and sat beside me.

So over the final two cables of water also I went as passenger and guest.

There were three men on the oars altogether and the stroke which they adopted was like a national anthem to them: storm or calm the tune never varied. It was an urgent thing to listen to, an easygoing thing to look at. They dipped the oars as often as a racing eight but they never swept them back at all; the most they ever gave the water was a short, not disrespectful push. It was much ado about little or nothing I told them on one occasion and they countered and claimed it was a corporal work of mercy: the slower the boat went, the drier the people!

If the rowing was peculiar, my position in the boat was

symbolic. I was sitting facing the stern so although I could see the *Sapphire* drifting away from me I couldn't see the landing place approaching. If I felt like singing, the song couldn't possibly have been 'I Know Where I'm Going'. But I did get a brief glimpse of my immediate future at one stage when my eyes followed my shoulder around and I saw Fr Blake coming down the gravel beach. His expression seemed set but he gave a little wave.

I felt nervous. Were his thoughts nearer to his face or to his hand? Was he glad of my coming or of his own going? Ought I to have got ready a little speech to say to him between beach and bungalow? Was there perhaps a kind of password that priests used when one relieved the other like soldiers on sentry duty? Fortunately before the inquisition trapped my confidence completely, the shore ran out to put a ramp under us and the punt grounded.

I stood up, looked around and there was Fr Blake smiling. Clearly all that needed to be said was 'Here I am and here's the salmon and how are you at all, Father, after all the years?' Miley wellingtoned ashore, tugged the punt clear of the crab shallows and left the prow standing at its full height above the dry gobs of the beach.

Out we all got with the steering of an elbow from Paddy aboard and the steadying of a hand from somebody else ashore. The somebody else in my case was Fr Blake – 'Here I am,' I said as I took hold of his hand – and he turned the help into a handshake, the handshake into a welcome and the welcome into a wish between the top of the gunwale and the bottom of the beach.

'There now, there's a happy landing for you,' he said, 'and many happy returns. Had a good crossing?'

'Lovely, Father.'

'Did it put an edge on your appetite?'

'It did indeed. I'll eat the head and tail of that salmon, if there's no cat around.'

'There isn't as a matter of fact. Aggie roasted him a few months ago.' My eyes must have squealed astonishment to him. 'Don't worry,' he continued. 'We weren't starving. It was an accident.

14

'Paddy!' he shouted towards the punt where the unloading was beginning, 'this young priest says he's starved. Hand him out that salmon.' Paddy did so as solemnly as if it was a scroll of ancient laws.

'Ye'll leave the cases and other stuff up later won't ye, Miley?' Fr Blake called.

'Yes, of course, Father.'

I protested that I could quite easily carry them myself.

'No, Father, you go ahead with Fr Blake. Do you want to shame us on your first day? We'll bring them.'

'First lesson in the island ways,' Fr Blake whispered, when I caught up with him. 'You carry their burdens and they carry yours.'

We moved up the beach. He did all the talking. 'Sickness or suitcase, the motive is the same. This is a kind of Christian republic and you're the Prester John. There are no guards here, no judge, no lawyers, no civil servants. You are the headman of the island and there can't be more than a dozen places in the whole world where the priest is that. If you say go out in a gale-force nine, they'll go out. If you advise them to change the seed to Aran Banners, they'll change it. When you tell them what the law of God is, they'll listen to you. You'll never meet people like these again. Don't be hard on them. And don't be easy, either: this is the good ground, this is where to get fruit a hundredfold.'

'You're sorry to be going away, Father, aren't you?'

'In a way, yes. But I'm glad too, because a change will do the people good.'

'That's not what I heard from Kathy O'Hally.'

'Kathy O'Hally is better at drawing pints than drawing conclusions. I'll bet she told you they're filling buckets of tears for me.'

'She did,' I said, astonished.

'She said the very same thing to me seven years ago about Fr Courtney. Look, don't think because there was nobody at the boat to welcome you that you're not welcome. It's just that they don't know how to deal with two priests at the same time. They think that if they come out in strength to greet you it will seem like rushing me away. Everything in the right order, first tears, then smiles. The old priest first, the young priest afterwards.'

Then, with a change as sudden as the change from the sliding pebbles to the solid road which we reached just then, he asked 'Do you like history?'

'Yes,' I said. 'Why do you ask?'

For an answer he shot a double salvo of shouts across my nose. 'Hey! Jack!'

It was my second lesson in the island ways and if formulated it would have said 'Don't watch pebbles when there are people about!' I couldn't see anybody at all until the buttress of a sunny wall left its architectural position and walked towards us.

'Jack Boyce, the island historian,' Fr Blake explained. He came towards us unhurriedly. What I noticed particularly about him was his hat. It was as big as something a woman would wear at a wedding; it had the colour of ferns when they rot in the autumn and it was as battered looking as a sombrero that had been kicked around the green room of a theatre for years.

'Jack,' said Fr Blake, 'meet the new priest, Fr Kiely.'

He lifted the hat about two inches off his head the way he would if somebody was being buried on a wet day. He offered me a hand with the slenderest fingers I've ever seen off a keyboard. 'You are very welcome in to us, Father,' he said.

I thanked him, and then Fr Blake said roguishly, 'You'll have to look to your laurels or your volumes or something, Jack. This young priest knows all about the kings of France, the queens of Spain and ...'

'The knaves of Ireland, I suppose,' trumped Jack, deliciously, beaming at the priest. Fr Blake looked like a boxer who leads with a neat but harmless left hand and is clobbered on the chin by a stinging counterpunch. The ring belonged to Jack. I liked him right away but perhaps he wouldn't have taken to me if Fr Blake hadn't acted as my second in a friendly exchange that followed.

I was sparring away satisfactorily enough when Jack asked me, 'What was the first thing you noticed when you came into the harbour?'

I felt myself walking straight into a KO but something inspired me to look to my corner. Fr Blake had casually moved around behind Jack a few moments earlier and there he was now out of Jack's vision but straight in the line of mine prompting the answer. He stretched his lips out and upwards in the shape of a currach and I could hear an 's' slipping between the teeth before the lips came back to a relaxed position. I had never read lips before but I could clearly see these ones building a castle in the air behind Jack's head and that's what I answered. 'The castle!'

I had often heard the expression 'his eyes lit up' but had regarded it as a metaphor. However, Jack's eyes really did light up and from the inside, like car lights being switched on.

'Did you know that the entire history of Capaill is contained in the castle?' he asked me but this time I knew it was a rhetorical question not a testing one and he went on, 'the island at peace and the island at war. The saints and the savages.'

My turn to ask a question. 'How's that?'

'Believe it or not, the doorway of the castle was originally the doorway in St Colman's Abbey. Cromwell's builder hacked it out of the abbey and stood it up again over there, with a barrack on its shoulders. 'Twas as if the devil stole the gate of heaven and set it up at the entrance to hell.'

'Aggie will be like the devil at the entrance to hell if we don't bring her that salmon soon,' said Fr Blake with a smile. So we excused ourselves and moved up towards the house.

On entering Fr Blake whispered to me, 'Be sure and admire Aggie's cream door.' What I remember about the dinner wasn't the salmon but that the subject of Sunday Masses came up in conversation and Fr Blake insisted that he would say the two of them himself. I had to wait seven years to know why. And even more surprising than his directing me to say a private Mass was his command to me to quit the island on Monday morning. It was a friendly order – 'You'll want to tell your mother about everything'; it was also firm – 'I'll be leaving on Wednesday morning and you are not to

17

attempt to return here until the half-past one boat that afternoon. I'll need the few days to myself, you understand.'

I did and I didn't: that packing up was a glutton of time, yes; that parting from Inish Capaill was a sorrow that was deeply felt, no. It was another subject that Professor Time would teach me.

TWO OTHER EPISODES, and the day ended. Two other half lies told, two other full friends gained. They were both similar to the Jack and the castle incident and in the first of the two, Fr Blake was at hand as before with reinforcements when my flank was being out-manoeuvred.

This occurred shortly after dinner. Aggie came into the living-room to clear away the dishes. I was standing at the window watching the rocks at the harbour entrance as the waves slashed into them. Fr Blake was at the other end of the room, patting his pipe affectionately. So Aggie was in between him and me.

'You're admiring the harbour, Father,' said Aggie.

'I am, Aggie,' I said, 'especially some cauliflowers down there, that are a lot bigger than any you ever drowned in a saucepan.'

'Cauliflowers?' she said, in a tone that wondered if the new priest was an even bigger joker than the last man.

'Yes, look at the waves. Look, there's a beautiful cauli sprouting now. Do you see it?'

'I do,' she answered, unimpressed. 'If you're going to live on that stuff you'll have no trouble paying your way. Spray is right cheap around here.'

'That may be, Aggie, but it's uncommon; it's beautiful like the harbour itself.'

She was mollified, and over-loaded the tray with a new confidence and verve. 'What was it you first noticed when you came into the harbour?' she suddenly asked me.

I very nearly blurted 'the castle!' Had I done so, it is myself who would have been demolished. Fortunately I gave a glance at Fr Blake and his lips were as busy as Aggie's hands. Rounded lips, an 's' hooked on to them and a finger pointing jabbingly at the floor could be the makings of one thing only, a house.

'The house, Aggie,' I declared. 'It stands out from everything else. The cream door especially. It's like a beacon from afar.'

''Twas I that painted it,' she said proudly, then lifted the tray with the flourish of a captain accepting a trophy and swept out of the room in triumph.

THE SECOND EPISODE occurred about half-past six in the evening. I mention the time because that's how the subject of Jamesy Prendeville came up in the first instance. My watch had been going crazily fast all the day before, and during the drive from home to Killeggan it had been gaining a lead of fifteen minutes in every hour over the run-to-rule clocks in the towns along the route. Then half an hour after I landed, it stopped altogether. If ever there was a meaningful symbol, that was one, and when I first thought of writing this book I was going to begin it by saying: 'Time stopped when I arrived at Inish Capaill; not that it mattered there'.

The point is, anyhow, that I had gone to the harbour window again and Fr Blake was standing beside me. An old man was walking along the road towards the post office. 'What time is it, I wonder?' I asked.

'Just before half-six,' Fr Blake answered without looking at watch, clock or sun-angle. 'Every Friday at this time Jamesy Prendeville goes for his pension. That's he on the road down there. He's a wonderful old man. 'Twouldn't surprise me a bit if he came up to see you on his way home.'

The obvious question to ask, and I asked it, was in what sense Jamesy was wonderful. Fr Blake's answer was something like this: 'Well, you know, he is that very rare being, a person who consistently regards God as a living reality. Now don't get me wrong. I'm not saying that the rest of the islanders are atheists but I am saying that He doesn't exist for them in any immediate sort of way. He is present only when the wind is strong and their fear is great or when a child is sick and then only as a kind of lull in the storm or a

19

doctor's prescription. Heaven and hell are as real to them as Cuan Mór or the Dirty Sound, but not God. God is a sort of mandarin that they keep at an immense and immensely respectful distance. Not so Jamesy. Jamesy wouldn't be one bit surprised if he met Him around the turn of any road. What's more, if he did, he would talk to Him the way he does in the church, which is the way he talks to everybody else. I don't know who said that prayer was a chat with God but I know one great chatter-box that God has.'

Ten minutes later Aggie came in to say that Jamesy was outside in the kitchen and he would like to meet the new priest. 'Tell him to come in, Aggie,' Fr Blake said. Jamesy arrived but he was as shy about coming right into the room as the door itself. Three feet, no more, was all he would advance. He took off his cap with both hands in a gesture of respect that made my conscience squirm. Fr Blake introduced us.

'We are as happy to see you coming in to us, Father, as we are sad to see Fr Blake going from us,' Jamesy said, dividing his sentence and his glances equally between us.

'You old diplomat, you,' Fr Blake teased. 'Where did you make that one up?'

'On the steps outside,' Jamesy admitted and he smiled, whether mischievously or innocently I couldn't say: either way his eyes reminded you of a boy's eyes, steady and bright. 'Every priest is the one priest.'

If a preacher had said that I would have called it mystical theology. Jamesy said it as unpretentiously as if he had announced that every penny was the same size.

'How do you like our island?' he wanted to know next.

'Well, up to now, I've only seen it small as a postcard but I wish every postcard was as lovely. The harbour is the one part of it I've seen so far, as big as God made it.'

'God doesn't make a botch when He makes things,' Jamesy said firmly lest I make a botch myself. Then the question that I knew must come: 'What was the first thing you noticed when you arrived in the harbour?'

On this occasion Fr Blake was behind me and I couldn't see what his lips might be drafting but ten minutes earlier they had built something holy and intimate and strong, something indeed like the small church outside the window where God's chatter-box chatted with God.

'The church,' I said. 'What else? As soon as you round the beacon your eye steers straight for the church.'

'I'm glad to hear you say so, Father,' Jamesy purred. 'You hear a lot of them tourists saying it's Cromwell's castle. Castle, how are you! You might as well say Cromwell's skull. And since Aggie painted the door outside there are even people who say it's the house here. Such nonsense. Well, I'll be off to the tea now. Excuse me for making so bold on ye. Long life to you both.'

'Twas clear from the smile he gave me that he went off, not to his tea but to a wedding feast in honour of a linking of hearts.

If Jamesy and Aggie and Jack were glad, I was glad three times over. I had accomplished the impossible in grammar: three firsts; and I had got myself in one day the three most wonderful gifts in life: three friends.

3

Housekeeper Extraordinary

THERE ARE CERTAIN AREAS of human relationships which consistently produce a rich crop of stories. The quarter occupied by men and their mothers-in-law never lies fallow even though the crop may consist at times of nothing better than chestnuts polished on the surface and rancid within. The teacher-pupils relationship is also very productive soil and there is never a school year without a harvest of bright and winning anecdotes flavoury as wheat itself. Priests and their housekeepers too form a section that has never known drought or blight since celibacy settled the Catholic clergy into it in the Middle Ages and they specialise in a slightly absurd kind of crop, yarns of the order of vegetable marrows and the like.

Ireland island has a longer memory than Inish Capaill but it doesn't tell any better stories about priests and their housekeepers than its little neighbour. In Fr Harrington's time, for example, the housekeeper came with him from the mainland. That was unusual because deaconesses seldom saw it as their duty to accompany apostles when the mission lay out of reach of the land. The crossing by boat intimidated them for one thing and residence on the island appeared to them on a par with living on a ship anchored nine miles off shore. Fr Harrington's Eileen, however, was young and frolicsome. She didn't mind a bit about dipping her petticoat in the well of the rowboat and if the island was an anchored ship itself it wasn't long before she knew every lively cabin in it.

When June came, Fr Harrington left the island for five days to make his annual retreat in Tirella. He had scarcely invited the Holy Spirit to dwell in his soul at the start of the spiritual exercises before Eileen had invited all her friends, boys and girls, to the priest's house for a dance and a party. They had a great night. They danced like Cossacks. They shook dust out of Fr Harrington's books as no cloth had ever succeeded in doing. A statue of St Alphonsus which stood on a plinth in the corner of the room completely forgot his principles and his composure, drummed his feet with the best of them and had to be restrained from leaving his plinth and joining the dancers on the floor. The kitchen was fogged up like an October morning. They had so many pigs' heads for the men, the place looked like the scene of a massacre. They roasted a whole lamb for the girls. Porter flowed like rain on St Patrick's Day. No night like it was ever experienced again on the island – which isn't surprising in view of the fact that the priest got to hear of it.

On his return, he hardly had his feet well out of his mainland shoes when there was a caller at the door. It was a pious vigilante with a report of the impious doings. The floorboards vibrated with passion under the priest's feet as the informer filled the sitting-room with noisy names. The kitchen steamed up once again when the lid lifted off his boiling temper as he was reprimanding Eileen. Nothing she said could convince him that the revellers had not only supped off his china but out of his pocket as well. All the resolutions that he had saddled so hopefully during the retreat, resolutions about controlling his temper, thinning his language and acting as the loving father of his people, fell at the very first fence and the shambles of his spiritual life goaded him all the more.

On the following Sunday at Mass the islanders heard a sermon which they never forgot. The text chosen was 'But you have made it a Den of Thieves'. Fr McSharry, his sermons' professor in Maynooth, wouldn't have approved of it on the grounds that the eloquence was not sacred but profane, but he would have commended one aspect of it. 'Always finish with a lesson or a practical application', he used to say. Fr Harrington did just that: as his last words on the subject he announced that the dues for the year were doubled forthwith in the case of every family that had a son or a daughter in his house that night wrecking his floors and eating his victuals.

Eileen was given the choice of sailboat or rowboat and exiled to civilisation, and thereafter Fr Harrington chose a housekeeper from the island for the duration of his stay as indeed did most priests. This arrangement had all the advantages of a fire prevention system: if no young torch of a thing came from the mainland then the island couldn't be put in a blaze, to quote Mrs White's famous phrase. But it had one great disadvantage, as Fr Leonard discovered: when the priest and the housekeeper squabbled she could do what wives did in comedians' tales – go home to her mother.

Fr Leonard and his Nora were ill-matched. He often regretted not having entered a Cistercian monastery where tongues were used only for tasting food whereas she kept up an unceasing chatter as monotonously as the sea. He liked his beef rare but rare to Nora was raw and raw meat was something that only lions ate so he got it well-done. He liked books and papers to accumulate undisturbed on his desk like sand at the mouth of a river; not so Nora who dredged them all away from time to time. He liked to build his own turf fire in the sitting-room carefully as a mason laying bricks but when he was out she often tipped a whole wheelbarrow of sods on top of it. If they had been married and in America, he would have got a divorce on the grounds of incompatibility of temperament.

There was never a day in their state of war that they didn't exchange small arms fire, as it were, and twice or three times in the year they engaged each other in a full-scale artillery duel. Nora invariably won these major battles by the simple expedient of a planned withdrawal which left Fr Leonard, it is true, in command of the field but a comfortless field without kitchen or commissariat. The tactics she followed were always the same. She used to detonate the front door with a tremendous bang, sally along to the east end to her brothers' houses, draft the unwilling men right away and order them to the priest's house to remove her bag, baggage and feather bed. The priest always held his fire while this operation was going on – Nora's brothers, after all, were non-combatants – and so when the last of her war gear, her mattress, went down the front steps unmolested, he was left master of his own house.

Master, but after one week miserable. The fire was neatly built but his day was in ruins. The desk was a pleasant chaos but his heart was in a state of disorder that he could find no pleasant adjective for. The house in the morning was as silent as heaven before the angels were created but during the day all the corners with mops and brushes in them shouted at him as he passed in or out. Worst of all, silence, a tidy fire and an untidy desk made for a very thin diet; and raw beef, really raw beef that is, didn't do anything to supplement it.

So in the end Nora always won. After seven days of scanty pickings on his plate, Fr Leonard's morale was lower than his squealing stomach and he was ready for peace talks. So he chose an emissary for himself from the east end – diplomats from other quarters were not acceptable to Nora – and he sent him to discuss terms. These were always the same: an apology from the priest, an undertaking to have her belongings transported back to the house at his own inconvenience and a pledge of permanent employment.

DURING MY OWN time on Inish Capaill, Aggie had a similar assurance of permanent employment but she got it not by haggling but by inheritance. She was handed down from priest to priest almost as a symbol of their jurisdiction over the island. She was rather like Tennyson's brook: priests might come and priests might go but she went on forever.

When Fr Blake returned to the mainland he left me two things, his Raleigh bike and Aggie. I saw no connection between the two bequests at the start except the conjunction but as time went on I saw a real connection between them which was in no way offensive to Aggie. The bike gave me the run of the island, Aggie gave me the run of life. She steered me, turned wheels for me, put brakes on me, eased my road and sounded warnings for me. She was never my housekeeper, always my homemaker. With Aggie around it wasn't dampness that came through the walls but the kind of concern that oozes out of them in the house where one has been born.

She was the kind of woman that you almost forgot to pay at the end of the month she was so much a part of yourself. 'Motherly' is the only single word which describes her and even the way I took her for granted was evidence of that motherliness. Monsignor Carroll used to say that all priests were spoiled by their mothers and that the priests who ministered in Capaill in Aggie's time were spoiled twice over.

This was the kind of thing that used to happen in Capaill 'in Aggie's time': A winter's morning. Dark blinds pulled down fully over the window of the sky. Rain hopping off the ground as high as shinbones. Nine on the clock for anybody who was interested in the time. Nobody was, except the eight or nine regulars who went to daily Mass.

On this particular winter morning the eight or nine were in the church, their fingers doing a circuit of the rosary beads, their feet doing a circuit of the Stations of the Cross or just sitting there inside the drenched tents of their raincoats, their minds doing a circuit of all the reasons why I was late arriving to say Mass; the unlikely charitable reasons up to twenty-past nine, and thereafter the uncharitable likely reason that I had overslept. As a corroboration of this, they took Aggie's absence from the church.

Wishing to put their theory to the test, two of them 'made bold', to use their own apologetic phrase, to go up to the house. They went around to the back door. To their astonishment, Aggie was up. She was sitting on a chair in the middle of what looked like a great clock of shoes polishing away like a soldier.

'Do you know what time 'tis, Aggie?' May Gregg began.

'Yes, I do,' said Aggie calmly, picking up a shoe from the ten o'clock position. "Tis going on for ten, I'd say.' Seeing that Aggie's fire couldn't be drawn on the perimeter, Kitty Mason decided to move right in on the main target area.

'Is the priest after sleeping it in?' she asked.

'He is,' answered Aggie in as matter-of-fact a tone as if

the question asked had been, 'Is the priest from the mainland?'

'I suppose he'll be down to say Mass soon': Kitty Mason again, deciding that a tentative statement might lure a better haul of words out of Aggie than her question had done.

The response was disappointing: 'It all depends,' said Aggie.

'Depends?'

'Depends!' Question mark and exclamation mark jostled in the air between Kitty and May.

'Yes.' Aggie was being provocatively monosyllabic.

'On what?' What else could they say?

'On when he wakes up,' answered Aggie, and she said it with a full stop, but the absurd simplicity of her statement roused the two women to further probing.

'You mean he isn't awake yet?'

'That's right.' Aggie was laconic again.

'And aren't you going to call him?' May was voicing her incredulity at Aggie's inaction up to now rather than asking a question about her future intentions but Aggie ignored the insinuation and merely answered the question.

'No,' she said.

'Ah, but sure, Aggie, sure 'tis ten o'clock.' Kitty Mason's impatience was upsetting her syntax.

'I know, but it's a terrible morning,' said Aggie. The time had come for an extended statement and Aggie made it. 'The day is only fit for the bed and the priest is tired so be off with ye now and don't be depriving the poor man of his small bit of comfort.'

There was never an anti-clerical female on Capaill yet so May and Kitty made for the door. When they got there, Aggie had a bit of advice for them. 'If I were ye,' she said, 'I'd go home for the breakfast. Ye must be doubled up with the hunger. And keep an ear cocked for the bell. When the priest is set to go down to the church, I'll ring it.'

Two hours later she was as clanging as her words. At ten minutes to twelve, the bell scattered rain like holy water east and west; and well refreshed by courtesy of Aggie, I went down to say the nine o'clock Mass!

When that bell rang, men all over the island folded stale newspapers over their chests, women held saucepans in the air over nothing and all alike said the Angelus. And so the first sentence was written in a new paragraph of the serial called 'Aggie and the Angelus'.

One of her jobs was to ring the Angelus bell at noon and at six but the kitchen clock did not always keep up to the pace set by Greenwich and indeed there were times when it tired of the incessant running and took a breather. The result was that the Angel in the prayer didn't keep to a very strict time schedule when he brought the message to Mary. However, the church bell was the island's clock, and, vagaries notwithstanding, its gongy word was taken before that of Radio Éireann or the BBC. Something of the Church's own infallibility rubbed off the bell rope on to Aggie's hands!

Brigette O'Farrell once saw her father change the clock on the dresser twice within fifteen minutes. The first time was when Big Ben growled six times on the BBC transmission and Mortimer crossed the room from the window where he was sitting to the dresser and gave a helping finger up the last seven steps of the hour to the minute hand. He resumed his seat. At a quarter past six Aggie rang the Angelus which was the same thing as registering a resounding protest at the inaccuracy of Mortimer's clock. Obedient son of the Church that he was, he got up, crossed to the dresser again and with the air of a man rebuking a forward child for not knowing its place and not waiting for its betters he pushed the minute hand back to the start of the circle again.

Acts of faith like Mortimer's were not unusual on the island but in an age of doubting Thomases, Richards and Henrys it is not surprising that some scepticism accompanied the tourists and the newspapers from the mainland now and then. People who put radio waves above sound waves and who put a foreign tyrant above the genial native ruler of their clocks began to comment to Aggie on the unreliability of her timing. This criticism gave her a complex about accuracy akin to a mathematician's and left her with the feeling that to be right she had to be exactly right. As a result, for a period of four or five months, she wouldn't ring the Angelus bell at all if she thought the time had slipped beyond twelve or six and during this phase she used to ask me what time it was as often as a city child out for a day in the country. Around Angelus time especially, a call used to come from the kitchen: 'Is it gone twelve yet, Father?' 'Is it after six, Father?' and with the aplomb of the announcers on Radio Luxembourg I used to answer, 'It is exactly twelve o'clock, Aggie' or 'It is now precisely six o'clock' when it was maybe ten past or a quarter past the hour. My standard, I must admit, was based not on meridians of longitude but on the necessity of prayer. My therapy was successful: Aggie recovered her composure, the island recovered its regular irregular bell-ringing and the believers – and they were overwhelmingly in the majority – went on believing.

Once, Aggie was pulling on the bell-rope as Paddy Mallon was pulling on the anchor chain of the *Sapphire*. 'Twelve o'clock already! I didn't think 'twas that late,' said Paddy to Miley. (Actually, it wasn't that late, as the few people whose clocks' ears were cocked to the radio could have told him; it was only a quarter to twelve.)

'We'll have to put all her pinafores on her,' said Miley.

That's what they did, dressing her in foresail and flying jib as well as main-sail. Once they had rounded the beacon, the wind was astern and they sailed her the way a small boy sails a toy boat, running before the wind and setting the main-sail as square as a towel on a washing line. They made great speed – there's no denying that – and the water boiled on each side of her as she ran hotly through it. The diesel engine too was in great form, not a wheeze or a blurp out of it, healthy as a rugby forward and pushing strongly. Paddy winked to Miley; that meant 'We're making good time'.

Miley patted the gunwale; the taps meant 'Not just good, but great'. The women looked at one another; the pale glances said 'What speeding they have; they'll drown us all'.

They tied up at Killeggan at twenty-past twelve. Fr Clarke, the Columban missionary who was home from the Philippines, was standing on the quay and when Paddy asked him what time it was, that was the answer he got: 'twenty-past twelve'. And it wasn't a guess on Fr Clarke's part; he punched at the air with a long left lead and called the time off his wrist.

Twenty minutes for the trip from Capaill to Killeggan! It cut the usual time by more than half and was the equivalent of a speed of twenty-seven knots. Incredible? Of course not. The Church, pillar and ground of truth, was there to confirm the time at both ends: the Angelus at one side and Fr Clarke's wrist watch at the other. It set up a record for the crossing which was never beaten and never will be beaten until the day comes when the westerlies will be strong again and the sail will be crowded and the engine will be excited and Aggie will ring the Angelus at twenty minutes to twelve just as the *Sapphire* is slipping her moorings and Paddy will tie up at Killeggan at a quarter-past twelve for a new record crossing of fifteen minutes!

Another time Jack Boyce was a ganger on a road-making job in the northern bog area behind Creagan. It wasn't a big gang – there were only four men besides himself – but it never developed into a small party. Jack had a conscience in these matters: he kept the men's backs bent and the picks picking, and the road moved on at a deliberate pace like the donkeys it was intended to facilitate. Jack's gang worked a five-and-a-half-day week, the half-day ending on Saturdays at one o'clock.

It was on a Saturday that Aggie took a hand in the affairs of the road gang. With Jack, one o'clock was one o'clock and as usual he had his watch with him to see to it that justice was done to the Board of Works with the big hand and to the workers with the small hand.

Now on the preceding Sunday, summertime had officially ended – the government finally deciding to take notice of the grey skies through the gaunt undernourished ribby trees – and all clocks had been put back one hour. Well, not all. Aggie's view on clocks was somewhat similar to her view on donkeys: when they were stopped you gave them a jerk but when they were going you left them alone. So, as she wouldn't halt a good-tempered donkey, hustle it back an hour's journey and then drive it forward over the same ground again, neither would she upset the way of the happily plodding kitchen clock. All that week, then, she was working not by sight but by subtraction, which was something I didn't know at the time and didn't appreciate even on that Saturday when just before twelve o'clock I passed through the kitchen on my way to hear confessions in the church. Aggie's clock held a reproving finger of one up to me as if I was an hour late for my duties but I knew 'twas only twelve so I promptly put it back to twelve. 'Aggie's clock is gone spurting mad again', I said to myself and went on to the church.

Aggie came back with the milk a minute later. The clock said twelve but for twelve Aggie read eleven and so didn't go out to ring the Angelus until the clock indicated one! When she did, the sound ran up the hill at its ease with the southerly wind behind it like a child going to school at the Creagan, it cleared the school-yard with a bound – something a schoolboy would wish to emulate – and onwards with it like a truant to the northern bog. At that moment precisely, Jack Boyce, having consulted his clerk of works, the pocket watch, was dismissing the working party. But when he heard the Angelus he countermanded his orders. 'I'm sorry for the disappointment, men,' he told them, 'but it looks as if the old watch is like ourselves, wishing the time away. It's only twelve yet,' and they went back to work for another hour!

NOT ALL THE stories about Aggie hung by a bell rope, by any means. One of them hung on a cat's tail, another from a tabernacle lamp. The cat was Fr Blake's. He brought her from the mainland with him during his final year and he made a great pet of her. She was a white Persian and he remembered enough of his Latin to call her Alba.

Alba had the misty blue eyes of a baby and ears that were pink and soft like the petals of a Bel Ange rose. She quickly acquired two of her master's interests: books and boats. Vanity rather than studiousness might have been the explanation of the first interest because she must have observed how Fr Blake had a number of his *objets d'art* on display among his books but there's no denying that her favourite place of pose and repose was on the middle shelf of the bookcase. She got the boat-watching bug – she hadn't any of the more customary feline types: Aggie saw to that – directly from the priest because he used to sit near the window with Alba on his lap and name out the various craft as they entered and left the harbour. After a while, even when Fr Blake was out and about she used to sit for hours at the window like a fisherman's wife waiting for the lobster boats to return.

The priest's garden was always aflutter with birds but Alba never molested any of them. 'Too well fed,' explained the islanders, simply. 'She does what the priest tells her', said Aggie linking the phenomenon with the benign influence of the priesthood. The islanders didn't resent Alba's presence or her prettiness but they did resent her price: they couldn't reconcile their idea of 'cat' with their notion of the value of a five pound note which it was said Fr Blake had paid for her. 'The weight of the seven winters must be softening his brain,' they concluded sadly. Not so Aggie who knew the ways of priests: 'They buy the strangest things,' she explained, 'little statues of blackies with no clothes on them, and razors that work without soap or water and chairs that go backwards and forwards and tilt up and down and swing round and round.'

Where the priests were concerned Aggie always followed the party line, and when Fr Blake said 'Vote Alba No. 1', Aggie implemented the policy quickly and completely. The cat got the same food as the priest, she was kept as spotless as a white rug in a sitting-room that is never sat in and, most important, she was always brought indoors out of the bronchial and promiscuous hazards of the night.

One night, however, Aggie couldn't locate the cat when she went pish-wish-wishing for her around the garden, and running out of patience and cat-talk she said to herself, 'Arrah, she'll come to no harm for one night.' That's where Aggie was wrong. During the night the Atlantic got very vexed and rain swept the island with the force of a fireman's hose. At seven next morning Aggie awoke with the terror of it all, thought of the cat, leaped out of bed and pitched to the back door. There was Alba at the doorstep as bedraggled as a tinker's rag. Aggie nearly lost her life at the sight. She grabbed the cat before the priest would see his darling drenched like that and brought her into the kitchen. The cat's legs poured water like down-shoots. Aggie's feverish mind could produce only one idea, heat, and heat suggested the calor gas oven. She put the cat in to dry her off. It was Alba who lost her life.

An even more celebrated accident was the affair of the shattered tabernacle lamp. We didn't have a sacristan as such in the church but Aggie's household duties bridged the small gap between bungalow and church and included the dwelling of the Lord as well. The church was God's sitting-room and she kept it like my own, sweet-aired and polished. The floor boards were as white as the deck of an eighteenth century flagship, and for spiders it was the most frustrating venue in all the webby world.

'Throw out that old sanctuary carpet,' she admonished me once. 'The Lord Himself must be sick and tired looking at it.' I agreed with her. It had probably been red at the time of the Russian revolution but was now very anaemic indeed. I bought a green carpet to replace it, a rich green like grass in a wet May and everybody was pleased, especially Aggie.

The mania she had for mop and style and order didn't extend to the sacristy itself which she regarded as a kind of church scullery, but that was the heel which the arrows of outrageous fortune pierced.

One morning when she opened up the church she noticed the tabernacle lamp spluttering, and deciding that the oil in it was too low to last until Mass was over she took it to the sacristy to replenish it. She topped it up from one of the heap of round tins – 'paraffin' it said on the blind side unknownst to her – inserted a new long wick and left it hanging like a linnet in a cage over the new green carpet in the middle of the sanctuary. That done, she secluded herself in the small organ loft, a privilege she had by virtue of her position.

I started Mass as usual about nine o'clock and everything went along normally as the rubrics would have it until the *Sanctus*. At that point just as I was saying 'Heaven and Earth are full of Thy Glory' the wick burned its unsuspecting way down to the paraffin; there was a great flash and a rending of glass and an explosion mightier than the hosannas of the heavenly host. Aggie bolted from her burrow and made for the hills; it was nightfall when she returned. The paraffin splashed down on the carpet and left a stain of the size and shape of a child's sketch-map of Australia. As long as that green carpet remains in Inish Capaill church, so long will Aggie's mark remain on the life of the island!

AGGIE WAS AFRAID of the fairies and in Aggie's mythology the fairies never spent a night in their own house but were always away from home squatting on somebody else's property. During the summer months she would lock up the church without demur but in the winter not even a declaration from the Pope would induce her to enter the building after dark. Neither the fact that I returned on countless occasions without having my legs twisted in a knot while extinguishing the shrine candles and lodging the timber beam in its iron jaw across the front door, nor the fact that Brigette O'Farrell, the teacher, returned from locking up on even more numerous occasions without having her head twisted backwards like some character in the Fianna could at all convince Aggie that the church wasn't full of floating spirits after the colours ran out of the stained glass windows.

For a while during Fr Blake's time she was sure that the fairies were making a recreation centre of her bedroom and they used to keep her awake all night, she said, thumping the floor and shinnying up the bedposts and laughing so heartily, the brushes on the dressing table danced. So Brigette went to sleep with her for two nights and never heard a thing. She was fairy-repellant, evidently, and she went home satisfied that the problem was solved. But on the third night they were as bad as ever, and 'they picked clean all the grease off the side of the candle', Aggie told Fr Blake on his way to Mass. That very morning, however, quite by chance, he met a fisherman who said to him, 'Doesn't Aggie stay in the bungalow at all now, Father? I saw her this morning at six o'clock coming down the hill from her sister's place.' All the noise suddenly went out of the fairy shindy. But not for Aggie who maintained that the revels continued nightly even though she was sleeping so far away from the bungalow she wouldn't have heard the bang if the place had been dynamited. At last Fr Blake gave her an ultimatum, 'either you stay or you go' and the result of that was to get Aggie to stay and the fairies to go.

Whenever I was out of the house, Aggie as deputy harbour-master kept a pair of binoculars aimed at the comings and goings in the harbour. From the arm of my easy chair and without a lock of her hair being seen, she could thrust those two long eyes right into the sailboat or into the punt and discover who was leaving or who was arriving, and from the luggage guess for how long. When I was away for a few weeks during the summer, she was always upset because she felt that the office of guardian of public morals devolved upon her! Fr Lavin who was home in Ballyheer on a holiday from Japan and who was doing *locum tenens* for me had a visit from her on one famous occasion. She complained to him about two naked women walking the roads. He hadn't gone very far with his enquiries when he realised that Aggie's 'naked' was akin to the Greek word *gumnos* and could also mean 'lightly clad'; what Aggie had seen were two English visitors in shorts!

Odd herself, she happily condoned oddity in others. A perfect housekeeper, she understood that every priest was a man and no man was perfect. She never attempted to break the shell of silence that surrounded her priests and when she spoke of them outside the house she spoke of them in general terms as a class and not as individuals.

Aggie talked very little, in fact, but she could cram a page of material into her favourite expression, a long drawn out 'oooh'. She would oooh with horror when somebody told her that Jack Boyce went home past the cemetery again at half-past two in the morning; oooh with astonishment when I used to tell her that I was going off on the bike again for the evening after being out already all the morning: on such an occasion she might follow up with 'rest yourself, Father, rest yourself. Where's the need for all that motion?' She had an oooh that was a childish joy at the anticipation of a marriage and an oooh that was a defence mechanism when I was scolding her about a phone call she didn't answer. (She never did answer a phone call: phones were a part of fairydom.)

But there was little scolding and little need to scold. Outside of home no woman has ever been so concerned to see me happy.

4

Festin of Ilen Festin

THERE NEVER WAS AN ISLAND that hadn't its quota of
inbred marriages and Inish Capaill had its share of un-
fortunate results of such marriages no less than the islands to
the north and south of it. But inbreeding had a happy result
as well: almost everybody on Capaill could claim relationship with the greatest islander of modern times, Festin
O'Toole.

There weren't many topics on which Jack Boyce and
Jamesy Prendeville saw eye to eye but when Festin's name
was invoked – 'mentioned' would be too weak a word to
carry the hieratic weight they gave it – Jack's and Jamesy's
eyes lifted on a parallel course to heaven: they were both of
them great grandsons of the man in the saga.

Most men who are famous are remembered for the manner in which they lived; considerably fewer for the way in
which they met their death; only a very few are renowned
for the way that they were born. Festin O'Toole's name oc-
curs in the short third list; and in the memory of Inish
Capaill he was the baby of babies.

Three miles to the south-east of Inish Capaill there was
an island called Ilen Festin. Nobody lived on it since the
sixth century when St Festin, who had to face no competition
in the naming of it, and five companions washed the sand of
Ireland off their feet and rowed out there to live a life of
hardship as uncompromising as the rock upon which they
built their cells.

One of the mysteries of religion not mentioned in the
catechism was how the monks kept soul and bones together.
Brother Bursar presumably would have been a fisherman
and when a boat would pass close by in good weather they
would have exchanged a tinkle of blessings for a sack of

meal but the main reason for their survival must have been the fact that their stomachs developed a slow puncture over the years and eventually became as attenuated as their fingers.

It is certain, anyhow, that the only tenants of the beehive cells after their time were the memories of the saint. Not even when Cromwell's grabbers made land scarcer than mercy did anybody from the mainland go out there to crop the lichen and die a slower death.

But where men starve, sheep thrive, and for a much longer period than they spelt their name with two 'o's and an 'e' the O'Tooles of Inish Capaill had been using the island for grazing. Each time the sheep were put on to it they must have thought it was Lent, but they, too, developed a monastic gut and no butcher was ever known to complain about the condition of the O'Toole sheep.

The clansman who owned the island, when its greatest drama was staged on it, was Petey O'Toole of Ceatharoo. He was more of a fisherman than a farmer; and looking out across the harbour from the gate of his house, on the winter day that arranged the set for the drama, he saw gannets spearing down the sky into the sea about a mile south of the white beacon.

'There's fish out there as sure as salt,' he said to his mate, Tim MacCarthy. 'Why don't we try for a score?' Tim was too mild-mannered a man to suggest a reason for not joining the gannets, so they agreed to gamble their sweat against their luck. If, at this point, Petey didn't remember he was a farmer as well as a fisherman, what followed would have been a day in the lives of two unknowns and not a day in the history of Inish Capaill.

Ironically, it was the sea that reminded him. It had the polished appearance that the sea has two or three times every winter and a schoolchild's ruler would have measured the swell. Conditions were perfect for landing on Ilen Festin.

Petey pushed a shout in the door before him. 'Leave what you're at, Ellen,' he said to his young wife, 'and come over with us to the Ilen.'

Easier said by Petey than done by Ellen. She was at the

time in the advanced stages of her first pregnancy. The consensus of opinion among the gossips was that she had another fortnight to go. Men are strange creatures; they act as if pregnancy was no more of an inconvenience than a heavy dinner. What begins as shyness about a wife's condition often ends as unconcern.

The trip to the Ilen wasn't intended to be an excursion to clear the kitchen smells out of Ellen's nostrils. The plan was that she would land on the island and check on the health of the sheep while Petey and Tim were fishing. Blood pressure was no more than a reeling in the head in those days and Ellen didn't demur.

The plan worked well at first. The sea was calm all the way from Capaill; not even once did Tim's head in the bow lift higher than Ellen's in the stern. Landing at Ilen Festin was no problem either: the cove was as quiet as a convent chapel.

'Don't worry, girl,' said Petey to her as they pulled out to sea again, 'we won't be long at all.' Ellen pulled her shawl tightly around her shoulders for company and moved up the slopes in the direction of the sheep. But as soon as the boat doubled the cliff at the mouth of the cove, Petey thought no more about sheep. It was the jumping sea east of Inish Garra that gave his mind bounce.

They had very good luck. They filled the boat. But if it was good luck, it was bad fortune, because they became so preoccupied with hooking and killing and counting fish that they failed to notice the black artillery advancing towards them in the south-east sky.

Suddenly a great salvo of a wind crashed around them and within five minutes the entire area between Inish Garra, Inish Capaill and Ilen Festin was spouting terror like a naval encounter.

Ellen! The thought of her dented their minds in the first rush of wind. They must get her off the island fast, and fast meant before the horses in the cove reared up on their hind legs.

Terror was a spur to the two men but the wind built ditches that they couldn't get over. When they gained two lengths, they lost one. They dug their oars into the sea like spades. They stretched their backs mercilessly. They threw out fish and then hope but they kept rowing and rowing. Their efforts were next to useless because the wind kept its huge knee dug into their backs.

They bled from the lips and their thoughts screamed around them. It took them five hours to row back to Ilen Festin and that was about four and three-quarter hours too late. The sea was in lumps around the island. The boat would have been thrown as high as Ellen if they had tried to beach it.

They could see her sitting on the cliff huddled in fear. They shouted a few scraps of hope to her about next morning early and she shouted back at them but the gale throttled her and they heard nothing of what she said.

There wasn't a thing they could do but put their stern to the wind and run in front of it to the white beacon and the harbour of Inish Capaill.

It was then the Great Debate began.

IT LASTED AS long as the storm. Every house on Capaill became a law-court and Petey was put on trial. In one the issue was whether Petey was guilty of cruelty in putting his wife ashore on Ilen Festin in the first place. In another the question was whether Petey was guilty of cowardice in not trying to land when he got back there in the height of the storm. In a third the matter to be decided by the kitchen lawyers was whether Petey was guilty of desertion in not facing out again the next day as he had promised Ellen or the day after that or the day after that again or the day ...

There were seamen like Colman Lacy who took the view that he could and should have beached the boat on Ilen Festin on that first evening. All that had to be done was to decide which particular wave you were going to ride on and then pull like a galley slave to keep up on its back. There was a considerable weight of water behind Colman's words because a few years before, himself and Chris Holland had beached a boat at Trá Gheal when the waves were as high as

40

the chapel roof.

Petey's friends said nonsense to that: Lacy and Holland had a whole bay to manoeuvre in; Petey and Tim Mac had only the width of a cove. To which Colman countered that a real seaman wouldn't need any more room to work in than he would get between the seats in a chapel.

The general opinion was that you couldn't say a thing couldn't be done until you tried to do it. Petey and Tim broke no timbers and they broke no bones which was proof enough that they didn't try.

There were people who demanded bravery of the order of madness, who said the fishermen should have rammed the boat against the cliff or stood it on its stern like a mummy's coffin.

It was no use telling these gallants that such an action would have been suicide because they asked in reply, 'Where is the suicide in risking your own life to save someone else's?' And they pointed out in a lower tone of voice, when there were no youngsters about, that Ellen was risking her life for him in carrying his child.

The bitterest accusers had the loudest voices. Common sense, which was a defence counsel, had a gentle manner and was scarcely heard and yet it had a good case. One whack off those rocks, it said, and the boat would have been like an orange box. There was only one way to save the woman and that was to save the boat and there was only one way to save the boat and that was not to try to save the woman there and then.

Besides, how was Petey to know that the storm was going to last longer than the night? He thought, naturally, that it was only a flash storm that would pale with the dawn. Who, of all the drenched and arguing men who carried the currach up the slip-way in Capaill harbour that night could have guessed it would be eight days before she would slap water again?

Eight days. Some of the old people argued they had known worse storms; nobody maintained he remembered one that kept their boats out of the water for so long.

During the first night the wind turned the corner at the

41

white beacon and for the next seven days it blew straight in the harbour, throwing cart-loads of seaweed over the quay wall day after day.

Day after day Petey came down to look and day after day he returned to Ceatharoo dejected. The arguing subsided as he went down and mounted in intensity again as he climbed the hill home.

There were people who said he should have gone out with first light on the second day. They said he had too many brains and not enough guts. They said the sea was only a lot of water after all was said and nothing done. It wasn't a million cross-cuts.

Colman Lacy claimed he'd have launched a boat from the quay himself only that his hands were tied by people's tongues; he had courted Ellen himself one summer unsuccessfully and it would have looked as if he were trying to prove she had made a bad choice.

Everybody except Petey asked the priest to agree with him but Fr Kennedy did what a priest must always do: he consoled the afflicted. He went up to Petey's house every day and he told him that storms have a way of passing and troubles too and that God was no less God than He had been sixty generations back. He put the mad thought of Ellen alive into the chalice every morning along with the wine.

On Sunday at Mass he committed himself to public debate for the one and only time when he remarked sadly that if people had prayed more and argued less the storm might have gone down long before. 'I don't say a miracle would have happened,' he said. 'Miracles are things that happen in other priests' parishes, not in mine. But God might have played one of His trump cards for us and, of course, He has a whole hand of them. If only we had been able to get Him to sit into our card school! Prayer is the way you cut the cards for God. Arguments only add to the wind.'

It wasn't really until then, the fourth day, that the islanders stopped reviling Petey and pitying Ellen. Up to then they had been considering her hazily through the heat of the debate. Thereafter they looked at the bleak facts of her position more and gave less and less for her chances of survival.

A strong man armed could have lived on mutton but what could a woman without even a penknife do? God had left no larder on Ilen Festin as He had done on other islands where trees collapsed under the weight of fruit on them. And even if she could have clenched her teeth against her own hunger, the child's needs would prise them open. Not even the Bedouin can feed an unborn infant on the air.

And hunger wasn't the only hazard. Even if a creel of food had been put under her chin, the weather itself, they felt, was enough to kill her. No woman could lean against it for more than a day.

There was a bit of shelter at the monastic settlement but only for a person who could contort herself. Summer had gone for the beehive cells and autumn too; the roofs had fallen in and only a low curve of wall was standing in one place.

On the sixth day when the people of Capaill were sure she was dead, a new and icy thought began to numb their minds: the gulls of Ilen Festin. There were hundreds of them there; they were fine weather fishermen and they would eat anything that was dead rather than die themselves. The women mostly agreed that God wouldn't allow Ellen to be pecked to the bone on a plot of land where only saints had ever lived, but the men who were wiser in the ways of carrion said that Petey would bring over only a very small coffin in the boat with him when the storm eventually died.

THE MOST EXTRAORDINARY thing about the storm was its sudden death. On the morning of the eighth day, a Thursday, the sea was still in a raging temper. At noon it wasn't even sulky. All the horses in the ocean went back to their stables without so much as a whinny. Nobody ever saw the sea to fall so quickly: not even a ladder would have fallen so flat so fast. It was almost biblical how it happened; it was as if Christ came down from Ceatharoo to say 'Peace: be still' and there came a great calm.

Petey and Tim Mac were off for Ilen Festin before most people realised the noise of the wind and waves had stopped. Every time they pushed water they leant so far back in the boat they were looking at the sky.

They made for the headland just north of St Festin's cell. The Giant's Nose it was called, and that's where they saw Ellen. Petey nearly broke Tim's back with the walloping he gave him when he saw her. She was running, actually running. They couldn't believe it. Petey let such a roar out of him it would have frightened a bull seal. All the gulls on the island rose up like a cloud of grey smoke.

Ellen ran to the tip of the Giant's Nose and stood there. To the two men she looked like the Blessed Virgin the way she had the baby propped on her arm.

Petey and Tim were pushing each other onto seats and off of seats; they were so excited they didn't know what they were doing. But eventually they got an oar each and they nearly wrenched the neck of the boat right off it, rowing around the island and into the cove.

Petey bounded up the rocks like a man who had springs in his boots. He was at St Festin's well before Ellen got back there. There was never speed till then.

Or tears. Or happiness.

ELLEN DIDN'T REMEMBER much about the first hours. There was a kind of blockage in her mind about them. 'But I remember,' she used to say in later years, 'I remember Petey's boat in the cove and it squealing like a pig. I thought himself and Tim would be kicked clean out of it every minute. 'Twas terrible to be watching them. 'Twas terrible too when they went away and I didn't know if 'twas the sea or the darkness golloped them up. I knew they wouldn't be back even if they got home: 'twould have taken St Peter to bring a boat in there.

'I stayed where I was sitting on the side of the cliff for a long time. I was afraid to move. The darkness was the worst part of it; it came in, threatening, from the sea like a big bird with black wings. I could see it getting closer and closer. I thought it would hit me. I was terrified.

'That was worse than the wind although the wind was

bad enough. Sometimes it used to catch me by the shoulders and twist me right around. I had to hold on to the ground with my two hands. I was afraid for the child.

'Then for no reason at all there was a kind of explosion in my mind and bits and pieces of pictures from the past leapt in front of my eyes. It was one of those pictures that saved me the first night.

"Twas a flash of my mother and myself when I was a young girl. I was going in the gate from school when she came to the door. "Ellen, girl," said she, "before you take off your boots run up the hill and see if you could find your father. He's up there with the sheep. You can hear them bleating." And as this picture faded didn't I actually hear sheep bleating somewhere above me and I rose from my place on the cliff and stumbled up the hill till I found them. They were sheltering behind a wall and I went in among them and they never moved. I squatted down beside them and that's where I spent the night.

'I didn't pray at all the first night. Really pray, I mean. 'Twas only a conversation I had between myself and my terror and the gibberish that I spoke was swept away by the wind.

'But when the morning came and the darkness lifted I saw where I was. Behind St Festin's wall. "St Festin, like a good man, pray for me," I said. I had never prayed to him in all my life before. He was only a name to me, the name of a rock with our sheep on it, the name that one of the Lacy's had, a name that you would maybe put on a boat. I never thought of him as a person who would have influence with God.

'But as soon as I realised where I was, it seemed the most natural thing in the world to turn to him, just as natural as it would have been if he came up the rocks in a grey robe with his fish and his books. And immediately I turned to him I felt safe; not just safe, either, but protected, as if there was somebody taking an active interest in me.

'It was easy to pray after that. "St Festin," I said, "You were a great man to come into this desolate place. The love of God was the boat that brought you here and the love of

God was the storm that kept you here. So God must love you back. Get His ear and put in a good word for me, please. If He wants me to stay I'll stay, but ask Him not to be hard on my little unborn infant."

'The wind roared the same way all that morning but my mind was as quiet as the crib. I went to sleep and when I woke up the sheep were gone and my hunger was gone; 'twas as if somebody fed me while I was sleeping.

'And that's the way it went the next day and the day after. The storm still leapt across the island but now I didn't notice it anymore than you'd notice the furniture in your own house. When I was awake I felt St Festin near to me and I chatted with him. Whenever the hunger came on me I fell asleep and each time I woke up I was refreshed.

"Twas on the fourth day that I got the pains but I had no fear at all. I felt like a baby myself in her father's arms, safe and loved. It must have been St Festin did it for me because the birth wasn't anything as bad as I had heard from people. I was in a kind of happy drowsiness and when it happened I hardly knew if it had happened or not. The next thing I know for certain is that I had the baby beside me and he was covered in a little robe.

'I nursed the boy on happiness for four days. I was in a round of love and I never noticed the whirl of rain at all. Then on the eighth day a great calm came over the island.

'There wasn't a sound of any kind for an hour, and then a sound came to me from the sea, the loveliest sound in the world, the clear chopping sound of oars. I ran to the Giant's Nose and there they were in the boat, Petey and Tim. Praise be to God, it was a wonderful sight.'

SOME PEOPLE IMMEDIATELY concluded it was a miracle and wanted to have St Festin canonised all over again. Fr Kennedy would only say that it was a game of cards in which the stakes were two lives and that Ellen had a really bad hand and St Festin played it for her and made aces out of her deuces and she won.

The baby was baptised that same Thursday evening in

the church of Inish Capaill and he was christened Festin. The crones were of the opinion that as he was the first boy he should have been called Michael after Petey's father; miracle or no miracle, they said, throwing away the grandfather's name was the same thing as throwing away the grandfather's luck. But crones are not always the best of prophets and Festin inherited not only old Michael O'Toole's direct puntful of luck but a whole ark full of it stretching back along collateral lines to Simon Peter and Jonah and beyond.

Indeed, luck isn't an adequate description of what used to happen when Festin shot his nets. Luck is the kind of thing that makes the deck of a fishing boat slippery once in a while but there never was a time when a man could step on to a boat of Festin's and not have to watch his footing carefully.

From the time he was a small boy he was fish mad. And it wasn't a question of like father, like son; it was rather the other way around. Petey never put on his sou'wester over a smile until he began to take Festin with him. Then all of a sudden the blasted nuisances of fish became the blessed creatures.

Even at ten years of age, no one on the island could score him fish for fish. He could talk to them in their native tongue and coax them on to his hooks. It was said he could follow their movements the way the police followed the tinkers.

Everybody knew what happened when Colman Lacy took him out with him. 'Where will we go?' Colman asked.

'The Pillars,' said Festin. The Pillars! More fish had been caught in the baptismal font than had ever been caught at the Pillars. But to please him Colman went. Inside two minutes Festin pulled in a turbot so glossy you'd have thought it was hand-painted. And that was only the start. Before they finished they had as many fish as there were beads in the rosary, the five Our Fathers going to Colman and the fifty Hail Marys to Festin.

As a man Festin taught every school of mackerel that passed south through the Dirty Sound or north between Capaill and Greek a lesson it didn't forget in a hurry. Wherever he sat in a boat, a volcano of fish erupted at his feet.

Whenever he talked about fishing his eyes flashed like young sprats. Before he was a man of thirty he had hookers of his own on top of every wave from Kinsale to Killybegs.

People forgot he was christened Festin; they called him Mananán after the Celtic god of the sea.

FOR YEARS AFTERWARDS, bits of the robe, in which the baby boy was dressed when Ellen woke up to the new reality of a living life beside her, travelled the island as relics and Jack Boyce remembered seeing a piece of it, ironed as flat as Mass linen, framed on the wall of a house in the east end.

And anybody who has a stout boat, and cares to land on Ilen Festin on one of the dozen or fifteen days in the year when that is possible, can still see in the half-shelter of St Festin's cell pieces of timber that no wave tossed into it. They are the remnants of the coffin which Petey O'Toole and Tim MacCarthy brought over from Capaill on the day they went to fetch the corpse of Ellen home.

5

Sage at the World's End

WHEN YOU MENTIONED history to the people of Inish Capaill they transformed the word in their minds into a picture of a man who walked across the fields at Duagh, his hands behind his back, his shoulders bent, his eyes on the daisies he had no wish to crush. Jack Boyce knew the history of the island in the way the others knew the price of lobsters and carrigeen moss. He knew of the monks who came with Colman searching for quietness in a bustling age, of the corsairs who came across the swaggering sea with Grania O'Malley, of Rory O'More charging like a brave bull and, like a brave bull, dying on the sands at Cloonabeg, and of Coote the Cromwellian butcher who herded the human cattle of three provinces into the island and slaughtered them there. History was in Jack's blood always and it had made him what he was, a man who thought about yesterday and had no thought for the morrow.

The islanders were never able to understand why, with his intelligence and his gift of the gab, 'he didn't do something better with his life' than act the butler to four or five cattle and serve as ganger on a road-making scheme through bog or moor on the rare occasions when the Board of Works had some money for the island or a politician was looking for votes. They could see no sense at all in his walking the sand dunes with his dog or sitting in the coves waiting for the tide to come in.

They forgot one thing: that Jack never grumbled and they grumbled all the time. He came to terms with himself and was happy. Lazy he might be, but not his mind. A beachcomber he was, but a poet too, the kind whose heart goes out to God on a blue day when the cormorants stand on the rocks like a strip of postage stamps, their wings etched evenly and precisely against the sky.

He had a naturalist's knowledge of bird and brine, field and fish, a romantic's love for them and a Hindu's reverence for them. 'Man, master of creation' was a theory that Jack disagreed with; he saw creation as an ark where all living things lived together as a family: man was an elder brother, no more. Jack had the same opinion of the man who struck an animal as he had of the teacher who struck a child: failing to reach rapport they fell back on rap. Between Jack and his cattle there was that kind of fellow-feeling which Christ blended into a lovely parable: he used never drive them but he would go up to one of them and say a little word and she would follow him and the others would fall into a line behind.

The only occasion on which I ever saw Jack worried looking – indeed he was almost distraught – was during a summer when the hay grew no higher than anybody's shin and the ancient island became aware of modern economics. With a big demand and a small supply it was a seller's market. Jack had always bought hay from Pat Gallivan and he foolishly supposed that business deals went along the lines of the latter half of the 'Glory be to The Father', so he made no approach to Pat until the time, as well as the hay, was ripe, early September. What Pat told him wrenched his heart an inch out of position. The hay was saved indeed but it was also lost; he had sold it over Jack's head and Jack's fences to Mattie Prendeville.

I met Jack that evening on the road to Duagh and he looked like a man who had been to a cancer doctor. 'What's wrong with you, Jack?' I asked.

The answer was such a long one that only an eighteenth century novelist would put it in direct speech and it all had to do with cattle and hay. Gallivan's chicanery was denounced in terms that Jack usually reserved for Coote who took prisoners on the general understanding that they would be spared and killed them on the grounds that no specific agreement had been reached.

The reason he needed the hay so badly wouldn't have won him any friends among the new-style rationalising farmers. They would have called it downright bad husbandry and loaded all the blame on Jack's own drooping shoulders. In the valley near the hills of Knock he owned a meadow to which he gave its head every year and, while the hay was putting on the inches there, he kept his cattle on the commons at Duagh. That year, however, for some reason that he didn't understand, his beasts didn't like the taste of salt in the grass of the dunes and they 'indicated to him several times that they would prefer to go up to the valley field'. So, to the valley field they went, Jack leading them as always, and down went the hope of hay.

After December he wouldn't have as much grass as would do for the cat's medicine so he was now faced with the lonely prospect of selling the 'herd' before the winter set in. It wasn't the fact that he would lose money that was squeezing the merriment out of his eyes, it was the fact that he would lose the beasts. 'I'll be fierce lonely after them,' he said. 'The winter will be black out entirely.'

Summers too would have been black, even if the sun's pendulum swung away north of the Tropic of Cancer, had the cuckoos not come back year after year to the kindergarten in the valley to learn their numbers. Jack had a calendar on the wall and it was the most complete school report imaginable on their progress.

Looking back through its leaves from April to August you might find, for instance, the square for Thursday 27 April with a 'C.A.' above it and a '3' below. Decodified, that meant: Cuckoo Arrived and he learned his one, two, three.

The page for May showed how bright a scholar the cuckoo was, that is on the days when he went to school because he was a fine weather attendant and didn't go at all on days of wind and rain. The fourth of May gave him 9 marks for counting up to nine, the ninth gave him 16, the sixteenth gave him 28 and the twenty-eighth gave him 37.

He reached his peak with an astonishing count of 52 early in June when the weather was at its pedagogic best. Then on, say, Monday, 19 June Jack would write the letters 'C.V.B.' between the one and the nine: that meant that the cuckoo's voice was broken and afterwards you could see that the bird wasn't so interested in school but was thinking of the journeyings of life.

Throughout July, Jack tabulated this adolescent instability and dissatisfaction until there was no performance good or bad to register at all. So in late July or early August, day after school-closed day, Jack sadly wrote in question marks after the dates and the question he was asking was answered by the cuckoo's utter silence and so, at last, Jack took his pen and with the sadness of someone writing R.I.P. he inscribed 'C.H.L.' – cuckoo has left – in an August square and called out a blessing across the rocks of Rinnaceol and the hills of Knock, the islands of Ireland and the waters of the Atlantic on the departed spirit of youth.

I often thought to myself that Jack was as much a pantheist as a Christian. He slept through as many sermons as he heard: his elbowing neighbours sourly remarked that if he went to bed on Saturday night he wouldn't have to sleep on Sunday but my explanation had to do with an idea regained rather than a sleep lost. I know I'm misquoting Wordsworth's stanza somewhat but I think I'm not misrepresenting Jack's attitude at all when I say that he would willingly have put his shapely initials to these sentiments:

> One impulse from a vernal wood
> May teach you more of man
> Of moral evil and of good
> Than all the preachers can.

He knew why the *roilleach* fed at Ceann Trá and that knowledge was more satisfying food to himself than a fresh pollock. Twice he was on Inish Leopard for the birth of a seal and each time the sight of it shaved all his age away and left him young and tender in mind. The nesting coots taught him the value of solitariness when there is some important task to be done and the jackdaws in turn lectured him on neighbourliness and the colours of the skylarks' eggs and the jays' eggs and the blue tits' eggs were an exhibition which God the artist put on every springtime, and every day that the sun shone, it shone with God's warm eyes.

Of the presents I got when leaving Inish Capaill, the most touching, because the most expressive of the man himself, came from Jack: an old tobacco box with two wild flowers inside. No man who walked with his head in the air would have found them. They were bee orchids, rare and lovely and named for the bee-marked bloom that nuzzled bee-like in the bell of them. Three days before I left he spotted them at Duagh where his cows were grazing but it was too soon to pick them, so, contrary to his principles, he coaxed the cattle into thinking there was juicier grass in the valley and moved them there. Happy then to know that the flowers would come safe he aimed a few arrows of stones through the field at Duagh towards the spot where they were growing, and, on the morning of the day I left, scout-like he homed in along his marks to the orchids and brought them fresh and honeyed with his wishes to me.

ALL HISTORY ABOVE the level of annals is, I suppose, subjective to some extent. A historian's literary style is itself a kind of interpretation. Whether Jack's style had in it more of the man speaking than of the men he was discussing, I can't say, but I do know that a discourse on the castle in the harbour sounded like this: –

'The first bit of building that ever was here was put up by a man called Don Bosco. Don't mix him up with the saint who looked after the little boys in Italy. Our Bosco was anything but a saint and he had boyos rather than boys around him. He was what you would call a buccaneer and I think that word is spelt with two "c"s but if you put in a "k" instead of the second "c", you won't be far out!

'There's some people tell me that he was an Italian, but that's ridiculous! What would an Italian pirate be doing up here in these empty seas and his own Mediterranean so full of ships they usen't to travel at all at night for fear of collisions? He was a Spaniard, really. They say a Spaniard is as good as a Connemara man for filling his belly out of empty furrows.

'Bosco had a chain across the harbour and there's no

cargo boat could get out to sea until it first paid its share of wine or hides or silk or whatever it was carrying to the man who lowered the chain. Nowadays, they call that sort of thing a sales tax but in Bosco's time 'twas called piracy.

'He was a big man, kind at home and savage on the sea and it took Cromwell's crowd twenty-two ships and fourteen days before they got the better of him. That's because he was fighting for neither God, king nor country like the fellows in Kilkenny but for himself. A man always fights best for himself.

'Three years after the Cromwellians took the island, a fellow called Sir Hardresse Waller and two colonels named Hewson and Sankey – wouldn't you know from their very names that the devil was the doctor who delivered them? – wrote back to England and said the best thing was to choke off the island altogether and they offered £500 and the ship *Elizabeth* to any contractor who would block the harbour once and for all. There's nobody would do it for them because there was far more than £500 worth of space to be filled and the ship they were offering as a lure was like Elizabeth herself when she was queen of England – blunt-nosed, yellowing and dressed up a lot better than her ugly frame deserved.

'So they changed their plans. When they couldn't strangle the harbour completely they decided to keep one hard thumb on its throat and they built this strong fort on the site of Bosco's castle instead. And as Bosco hadn't amassed enough building material for them on his own they added to it from Grania O'Malley's store across the harbour. That meant they knocked down two castles to build one. 'Twas a good job for them that Grania was in her grave or they would have been measuring the depth of the harbour with their noses. No woman likes to have her hat knocked off and that's what they did to her when they sliced her castle off the Dún over there.

'Anyhow, they put it up and 'twas a fair big building, eighty feet one way and forty-five the other. They were on sloping ground so if you had a long piece of string with a stone at the end of it and threw it over the walls, you'd find that they are only twenty feet high on the south side but they are a good discouraging fifty feet on the north side. As far as I can make out, they had nine rooms and thirty of those narrow windows where the muskets could poke an eye out. In the middle of the yard they had a well, but by the way they treated the prisoners who were brought here, you would think they had no thirst on them but a thirst for blood.

'When 'twas cut-stone they wanted for the doorway, the bastards – "saving your reverence, Father –"'

'Too good a word for them, Jack. There were good men in history who were bastards.'

'True for you, Father. Well, the dirty bastards took away the whole doorway from St Colman's. Imagine, stealing an eye out of a saint's head! How could they have any luck after that? There'll be a curse following them in hell for the rest of their restless days.

'They had a lot of guns here, mind you. Seventeen guns. They had fourteen small cannon for the close-in work and three long cannon out there on the rock where the beacon is now. "Gunrock" we still call that place. Those big ones could knock the wind out of a ship's sails a thousand yards away, and the sails out of the ship itself with a good second shot.

'Those were bad times for Capaill, the times when Cromwell was a good word in the castle. When a prisoner went into the cells 'twas like a sod of turf into the fire: he came out as ashes.

'In the fields near Steevie Ring's house they changed the colour of the grass. Coote gave Colonel Honnour the order to clear the island of what he called "disaffected persons" and the best way that Honnour could think of to carry out the order wasn't to get a fleet of boats and ship them away but to get a company of soldiers and shoot the problem down. Honnour had one of those strange Cromwellian names, and you must say this in his favour: that he had the good grace to spell it with two "n"s. The only way you could connect him with the virtue of honour would be to misspell his name.

'All the same he was a religious man, it seems, because around the time he was placing cannon on the rocks he was also installing an able, pious and orthodox minister of the Gospel on the island. That's the only Cromwellian I ever felt sorry for, that poor man who came with a Bible to a place where they judged his book by the cover and the cover they saw was a cover of iron.

'They were bad times indeed. Jamesy Prendeville swears that even the fish left and they have been nervous about coming back here ever since. I wouldn't know about that, I never did much fishing myself. One thing sure, though, is that God hadn't much patience with those Roundheads and they were all gone by 1660. You'd imagine they would know better than to think they would fare better than other black-guards in history before them. A king followed the killer of a king and that was that.

'Castles are like furniture, you know. They never remain in the hands of those they were made for. They are always changing hands. So the castle here went from the Cromwell-ians to King Charles and from Charles to King James and from James to King William, and after William, when there was nothing and nobody to guard against anymore, it fell into the hands of its final owner, Time. And I'd say by the look of it that Time won't give up its lease for a few hundred years yet.'

JACK'S HISTORICAL ARCHIVES were a biscuit box. One day he said to me, 'Next time I meet you I want to show you an article about when the Madonna of Györ was in Capaill.' A few days later his cows and my calls brought us together again and he said, 'I have that article for you.' But instead of putting his hand inside his coat to fetch it out, off with him across the fields at Duagh to a clump of nettles. He bent down and pulled out a small tin biscuit box with a spread of sweet peas on the cover. The action reminded me of that snatch of Shakespeare where it says 'Out of this nettle ... we pluck this flower ....' Inside the box were various crumbs of old manuscripts and yellowed clippings. All of them as fresh as sealed biscuits and as colourful as flowers to Jack. Among the number was the account of how Our Lady of Galway

56

became Our Lady of Győr.

Bishop Lynch of Clonfert, it appears, escaped from Galway with the Weeping Madonna during the siege of 1651–1652 and lived for some months in Capaill. But when he heard that the Cromwellians were fitting out a flotilla to occupy all the islands, he became afraid that his precious picture would end up as a minute of coloured flame in a halberdier's bonfire so he left Capaill for the Spanish Netherlands and wandered Europe with the Madonna until he came to Győr in Hungary. The people there made him and his picture welcome and that is where it has remained to this venerating day.

Jack could spout history as well in my chair as in Cromwell's castle or on the Duagh commons, and I always loved to see him call and have late supper with me and to talk flesh and bone, fields and waves on to my table-spread maps of the island, sometimes until the Plough tumbled upside down in the night sky.

When I went to Capaill first, nobody told me that Jack made his social calls rather late. 'I'll be over to see you tonight and we'll have an old chinwag about what's under the skin of this place,' he said the first time he gave notice of motion. Where I was reared 'night' meant from eight o'clock or so onwards but with Jack, night was night in the geographical sense. I didn't know that, however. Half-past eleven came and I concluded that a sick cow must have prevented him from calling so I went to bed. That's where I made my mistake, because he did call after all, at five minutes past twelve – so Aggie told me next morning – and was very surprised to hear that the priest was gone to bed so awful early!

I never repeated that error and over the years that followed Jack reciprocated my goodwill by arriving somewhat earlier and, in the final year, the strong shoulder used to make the outer door vibrate and the oilskin coat used to hit the hall a clatter at a quarter-to eleven. I loved to see him smoking that pipe of his: there was a grandeur of gesture about it that matched the man as he pushed it back to his tonsils and hollowed his cheeks in the pull of it.

The only time in the life of the island when Jack came near to notice outside of it was when a geologist paid us a visit. A lot of people couldn't understand why he went to so much trouble drilling and poking for 'biteens of stone' when he could have got all the stones a queer hawk would ever need simply by walking to the North Beach. The explanation that he was searching for specimens and not stones couldn't convince them that the lack was in his head, not in theirs.

Anyhow, in one of Jack's fields the geologist discovered rock of great interest: he chipped off a bit of it and washed it and weighed it and analysed it and told Jack that he was the owner of soapstone of the highest quality. Seamus Lenny who owned all the hill of Knock behind Jack's field complained, 'My land is all rock and they aren't worth a spit and you have only one rock and they heard about it in Canada!'

In fact, Jack's mineral wealth was never exploited and I know that he was glad. He greatly preferred to have his soapstone where God put it than to have all the money in the ransacked world. And if they came for the soapstone they would have trampled the field, and if that had happened how could the bees have nuzzled in the secret orchids?

6

Walkabout

THERE WAS A TWIST in the road leading to the eastern end of the island which was always referred to as Bottle Point. I don't suppose that the breaking of a bottle has been commemorated in a placename anywhere else in this bottle-breaking world but there was a good reason for it in Capaill.

During a wake one night, a man took too much drink and started acting the goat. In a little while, complete identity followed caprice: the poitín put horns and hooves on the fellow and away with him out the door with a bottle and up the hill bounding from boulder to boulder like an enraged puck. Nobody followed him; the old principle of the goats applied: where he can go up he can come down.

On the following day it was something else came down. As the funeral loped along past Loch an Teampaill, a bottle filled with sand came grenading from the rocks above the road and exploded at the feet of the people walking after the coffin. 'Tis a wonder to the two hundred who were there that there wasn't a second corpse to bury. And if that had happened, no doubt there would have been a third as well!

A few hundred paces beyond Bottle Point was the cemetery and the ruins of St Colman's Abbey. There were two ways of looking at the two of them, God-acred behind the one wall. Either the Abbey, because it was dead, was in the city of the dead; or the dead, because they were spirits, were allowed to penetrate the monastic enclosure.

In Ireland only the very odd person can be bothered about attaching himself while alive to an eminent man but people generally want to be buried near one. They wish to rest where monks worked, to sleep where holy men were awake o'nights, to wait for an angel's trumpet where an abbot's hand-bell rang.

Inish Capaill for all its separation was very Irish in this. In three hundred years no islander was ever buried anywhere but where monks lived for a thousand. Once when I suggested the advisability of a new cemetery they looked at me as if I were propounding a new morality. They took the view that what you needed on Judgment Morn was a great battalion for company, and, with the world doddering the way it was, a new cemetery mightn't have a long enough life to give you that, and besides, the Abbey gave you not only a mighty battalion but an élite one: marching with monks the Lord wouldn't notice if you were a little bit out of step!

The monks came to the island in the middle of the seventh century. Colman brought them. He was looking for a place where God wasn't deafened with noise; he found it between hill and hill, ocean and lake. His companions were a mixed lot, some Celts and some Saxons but as soon as the building of the monastery was finished the wrecking of harmony began.

Some people say politics were responsible for the Saxons eating at one end of the long table, the Celts at the other. Not at all, other historians tell us: it was a labour dispute, purely and simply. The Saxons as immigrant workers got most of the heavy tasks and began to speak of the lazy Celts; this got the Irish tempers working harder than their pickaxes and Colman had to come between them as a peacemaker and peace meant separation. He took the Saxons to the mainland where he resettled them and then returned to Inish Capaill to found a school and listen between psalms to the praying of the sea for the last eight years of his life.

For almost exactly a thousand years afterwards the Saxons stayed away. Then in the 1650s they returned with round heads and straight lunges and it wasn't the building of abbeys they were thinking of but their utter destruction. The present ruins are a good example of their efficiency at demolition work.

Actually, several churches were erected on the site of the original foundation between the time of Colman and the time of Coote. The one to which the Cromwellian crow-bars gave a congregation of rubble was built in the thirteenth century. It was sixty-five feet long by thirty-three feet wide and was divided into two sections, nave and apse. It was from here that the beautiful doorway was taken away by the un-aptly named Colonel Honnour and inserted in the new castle at the harbour mouth.

Starlings are fond of the ruins; anytime I went there they were sitting on the gable like dragomen on a pyramid and chattering, all against the rule of silence, inside in the church. There were times too – in all honesty I must admit it – when the nettles were a disgrace to both abbey and cemetery: un-monastic and unascetic they looked over the wall to the out-side world and they had such hardy lives that massacre after massacre couldn't put an end to them. The rabbits too loved the enclosure and many of them claimed sanctuary there. No man would do so unsanctifying a thing as fire a shotgun in the cemetery; the dead might be awakened before their time!

One corpse indeed was disturbed about a hundred years ago when a grave digger opening up an old grave for a new burial found the body of a woman in a perfect state of pre-servation. He crossed himself, closed up the grave again and that was all.

He didn't know that there was a Congregation in Rome which would have investigated this discovery if requested in which case the anonymous corpse could have become a noted saint. All that mattered to him and to the other island-ers was the knowledge that on the last day they would have one of their own kind as well as Colman and the monks to give them a helping hand out of their graves.

Ascetic indeed the lives of the Celtic monks were, but judging by the siting of their monasteries all over Ireland they didn't mortify their eyes: they never deprived them-selves of a good view!

Always where monks settled there was the bend of a river to speed the eye or a bright buckler of an ocean to steady it, a hill to lift it or a lake mattressed with water lilies to rest it. They were right, of course: to them psalms weren't words they read but a life they lived. There was little point in chanting 'Come and see the works of God' unless they were themselves in a place where they could see them. There was little sense in bidding the mountains to praise God unless they could get to within echoing distance to tell them. And how could they get the surge of God's power into their singing unless they knew the roar of the waters and the breakers of the sea to which they likened that power?

The monks of Capaill chose their site well, in the lap of a valley with the arms of the hills right and left hugging it, the lake behind it, and in front grassy slopes, a stretched bow of beach, an island smoothly ramped by the winds, and all around the God-great sea itself.

The island is called Inish Leopard and ten minutes' walking brought you from the Abbey down through the fields and on to the beach from where you crossed to it. I was on Inish Leopard several times and always by walking there: it isn't every island you can visit on foot! Not dry shod, of course; if you were lucky you got in dry-kneed and you got out dry-thighed. You could do it only on a day when there was what they called 'a good strand', that is, when almost the whole seafloor between Capaill and Leopard was stripped of its covering of water.

Every time I went in there I set off an explosion of fish and almost invariably I met Peter Lenny coming out with a sack of turf. 'Don't stay in there too long, Father,' he used to say to me, 'the sou'west will blow up the flood very fast.'

Lenny was always advising people about the hazards of walking to Leopard and one of the laughs that went all around the island as loud as donkey's neighing was when he was caught in there himself and marooned for eleven hours, hungry, cold and forced to work his *sleán* for a longer period than he had ever moved it in his life before. He signalled to two currachs for rescue but they pretended to see only friendliness in his gesturings and waved back animatedly to him themselves!

The gulls always objected to my intrusion when I went in there and once two ravens flying very low squawked nastily all around my head, but I understood their feelings. I would have been just as angry myself if a bare-legged outsider walked on to my deserted island.

Once upon a time, however, Inish Leopard was not deserted. Three families used to live there when people were many and land was scarce. Indeed, land was so scarce in Capaill at the turn of the century that cows grazed only on the commonage or else between the drills of potatoes, and the young boys used to be put sitting in the fields all day to see to it that the cows didn't stray out of their own lanes. But during my time the only things to be seen on Leopard were the well that nobody drew water from, the small navigation light that looked after itself, the ridges in the fields where the Donnellys set their last potatoes in the spring before they all went off to America, and Lenny's handiwork: sods of turf heaped up into little beehive cells or sizable rotundas with pilasters of stones surrounding them.

FOR EVERY ONE occasion that I walked on Inish Leopard I walked on the beach opposite it one hundred times. It had the gentlest declivity on Capaill, it was the safest to swim from and it gave you a sofa in the sea-birds' refectory. It was divided in two by the little stream that introduced Loch an Teampaill to its distinguished cousin, the sea. On one side of the dividing squiggle was Trá Eoghain and at the other side Ceann Trá. The Ceann Trá stretch was the roilleach's dining-table, a table that got bigger and bigger, like something in *Alice in Wonderland*, as the tide ebbed. From the start of the ebb to slack-water was the roilleach's feeding time. He would scoop up shellfish, siphon the delicacy out of them, trample on the leftovers and then move further out the strand. The sea-pie, or oyster-catcher as he is known to English people, has a straight orange bill, very chic black and white plumage and pink feet. He is a beautiful bird in flight: his bill is stream-lined like a mach 2 jetplane's nose and his wings have the exaggeratedly beautiful markings of a new nation's air-force.

On Capaill they always called him the roilleach and Jack Boyce told me why he would walk into the water only as high as his stomach and not an inch further. It seems that the roilleach was a splendid swimmer once, and the seagull, who was then only a wader, was quite envious of his skill.

'Give me a loan of your flippers,' he said to the roilleach. 'I'm sure I could swim well if I had your equipment.'

The roilleach looked sideways at him hesitating.

'It's only for a loan; I'll bring them back to you,' urged the seagull.

The roilleach was drowsy after a big feed of oysters and his mind wasn't functioning clearly.

'All right, so,' he assented, slipping off his flippers and giving them to the sly one.

Alas, for his generosity! The seagull never returned the gear. And that's why the roilleach isn't web-footed and can't swim and that's why Mayo people speak about a loan which will never be paid back as the loan of the swimming gear that the roilleach gave the seagull.

As well as the stream, another thing which connected the lake with the sea was a trickle of religious history. Just after the Famine, when many people left their holdings, three members of a sect known as the 'Dippers' arrived in the island and acquired a cottage near Loch an Teampaill. Adult baptism by total immersion was the main tenet in their teachings and they intended to use the lake as their baptistery.

This was, of course, at a time when ecumenism was un-known both to dictionaries and to men's minds. Proselytism, however, was a word which had a nasty taste even when it came out of a soup-tureen and the people of Inish Capaill decided that nobody was going to reach their hearts through their mouths. So, after a few hints, obvious as crow-bars, had failed to dislodge the Dippers, six men from the east end, scarfed like bandits, broke into their cottage late one evening and overpowered them in a short, unfair fight .

Wrenching the Dippers' arms behind their backs, the six marched them down along the river bank to Trá Eoghain where, it being the swimming time of year, they stripped them naked and hustled them into a rowboat that was mod-estly waiting there. Then, John Foley who had heard them preaching once or twice and knew their style of utterance pushed off from the shore with a long oar and a text of his own making: 'Who so dippeth, shall be dipped!'

They rowed them out as far as Leopard Head. 'Now do you see that island out there at the edge of the evening?' John asked them, pointing towards a hunched shape of rock about two miles away, 'That's called Davillaun. The next time we will bring ye for a spin, we will take ye that far and ye can swim back in your own time. But this evening, because ye mightn't be in trim, we are only going to bring ye this far'; and without another word they tossed the three overboard, as if they were mackerel in a year of glut .

They had to fish one of them out straightaway because he went down like an anchor and they were lucky men that he didn't get fluked in seaweed down below. They hauled him in over the gunwale like a sack of meal into a cart. When he recovered his senses fully he knew for the first time in his evangelistic life what total immersion really meant!

The other two struck out for shore but it was from the rowboat that they also landed. The tide was ebbing strongly and half way in they were exhausted and turned over on their backs with pleading arms. On the very next day the mission to Inish Capaill withdrew from the island: lakes were all very well but the Dippers didn't feel equal to the ocean.

This wasn't the end of the incident, however, because they naturally put in a complaint to the police. John Foley was arrested and tried at Clifden Assizes; it was his red hair not his companions that gave him away. He was found guilty of assault, kidnap, murderous threats and conduct calculated to cause extreme embarrassment to his victims. He was in jail for two years and during that time he met another prisoner, the famous Fr Rattigan, who like himself was on the wrong side of the prison gates because zeal for the house of his faith had led him to devise a felonious prank.

It seems that Fr Rattigan, Bible reader though he was, was irked to find that members of a Bible Society were going around the adjoining parishes with barrows full of free bibles. The distributor-in-chief was an English lady who travelled about the country on an ass. Fr Rattigan's district of Roundstone would, he guessed, be the next to see the Greeks bringing gifts, and Helen Trotter – with a name like that how could she avoid having an ass for a companion? – riding headstrong like Balaam of old along the narrow roads.

Fr Rattigan knew he couldn't get the ass to emulate Balaam's by lying down under her, speaking to her and inducing her to go home. His plan was just as effective, however. He fetched a jackass, kept him in his stable without food, drink or the sight of an ass for a whole week and then when the lady arrived in Roundstone let the jackass loose! Poor Miss Trotter got a shock that nothing in her Bible-reading had prepared her for, and Fr Rattigan got a jail sentence. But he returned to Roundstone later on; Helen Trotter never.

John Foley too returned to Inish Capaill to shove off other boats with a long oar at Trá Eoghain, to toss out lobster pots with a Dipper-splash at Leopard Head and to swim in long arcs at Rinnaceol.

Rinnaceol was where the men from the east end always swam. It was a small courageous promontory beyond Ceann Trá. The boys bathed from a glowing little sandy cove shaped like a Celtic neck-piece called Porteen on the other side of the promontory. So the men jumped from the top storey, as it were, and the boys walked in at ground level and stayed at that level till they left school. Man or boy, brave or bashful, they all swam in the old days; there wasn't one of them who couldn't swim for his life or, if need be, for his livelihood.

Jack Boyce remembered one evening late when he was in a fishing boat a fair distance off shore at Pollnapollog. He was out for the fun of it in Steve Geoghegan's boat. He was about twelve years old at the time. The bow man had just lowered the grapple and they were all going to their various lucky seats when Steve who was rummaging in the stern used an expression not fit for a twelve year old's ears. The extenuating reason came next: 'I'm after forgetting three of the lines. I left them in the house.' It was a situation that called for action not curses or confessions and Steve produced it. In about six movements of his arms and legs he peeled off, dived over the side, swam to the shore, ran naked through the darkening fields to his house in Cloonabeg and came back the same way with the fishing lines around his neck.

Things have changed as regards swimming on Capaill. Nowadays the men look at Rinnaceol and think incredulously of the giants of old and it's a far cry from the days when a lad, who was sent to milk the cows on the commons at Duagh, didn't return with the pails on a summer's day until he made the water in the Porteen creamy with a swimming form. Now they say "Twould paralyse you.'

There's the makings of a conclusion there somewhere, but a person who isn't as fond of them as I am can formulate it.

SWIM OR NO swim, Rinnaceol was the place to see Davillaun from, if what you wanted was to witness a place mocking its own name and lying in public. Davillaun means 'Two islands'; one was slightly north of the other, but from Rinnaceol they defied the findings of simple addition, one and one making one. They were like the two cars of a tram welded together by the angle of vision.

From other viewpoints the islands were their candid selves: two Siamese twins separated by virtue of a long and difficult operation performed by the sea.

The strait between the two bits of Davillaun was called the Dane's Gap. The story is that in the ninth century, in the twilight of a great era, a Danish raider cargoing plunder from the monasteries was spotted by an Irish vessel in the twilight of a November day. Exhausted the seams of Ireland's golden age might be in the minds of artists, but not the supply of golden cups and coronets in the holds of serpent ships. The Irish galley piled on sail and thumped in pursuit of the Dane. Cupidity is a greater energiser than husbandry and the Irish oarsmen with the trickle of gold rolling down their sweating arms began to gain on the Northmen.

But the winter night was faster than either and overtook them both in the race. After that happened, the Irish skipper navigated by sound: he took his bearings from the thud of oars and the snapping of sails. The Viking captain's compass was something that was dropped into every boy's cradle in

Scandinavia, a thing called daring.

Early in the chase, with the gap between the Irish galley and himself getting less, he had noticed the gap between the twin islands on his quarter. Come wreck, come wrath he decided to sail through that gap. As he came up to it in the pitch of the night and the ocean, he gave the order to his sailmaster, 'Luff her to, but don't shake the sail' (a phrase that sailors still use in Inish Capaill, when they want to bring a pookaun's prow into the wind, always adding 'as the Dane said').

The Dane pointed his long ship into the wind and the seamen throttled the canvas; there wasn't a whimper out of rope or wood. They edged, silent as their fear, through the gap, and as they did they lightened ship by tossing a lot of freight into a gully on the island.

The ruse worked. The Dane gained half a league and got clean away. By the time the Irish captain had rounded Davillaun, he had no sounds to steer by except the sounds of wind and sea, and they brought him everywhere and nowhere.

The booty which the Dane unloaded got two young lads from Capaill a hiding eleven hundred years later. One of them was Billy Laselle. The other was Brendan Ward, the most enterprising youngster on the island: he was always bleaching carrigeen, turning hay, reporting the ledgy whereabouts of missing sheep, operating a goods transport service for pensioners who no longer kept donkeys, and invading the private nooks of seashells with an eye to extracting sixpences from tourists' pockets. The American uncle who will send Brendan his fare to New York won't regret it.

On this particular day, Billy and Brendan were taken by their fathers in a currach to Davillaun to cut turf. They were given sleáns and instructions and the two men went off lobstering. Hours later, when the last of the pots were pulled and the evening clouds clawed a lobstery sun, the boat returned and the two lads stepped in, and off with them homewards. There was a brightness in their eyes that not even bellowed turf could have put there.

'Did ye get much done?' Billy's father wanted to know.

'Oh, we did. We were wet working,' Brendan quickly

answered.

On the following day, the pair of them were landed with their sleáns again and once more they got wet working but it wasn't with perspiration but with gully water. What were they doing only opening a trench out of the gully to drain it and find the Danish loot!

Their minds got buried so deep in the cutting that they completely forgot the upper world of fathers and currachs. But that is an attitude of mind you can't expect fathers to reciprocate when you are ashore on a barren island and they are lobstering only a mile or two away.

The evening came, and with it the currach. It nudged the landing place but the boys didn't hear it. The two men climbed up the rocks but the prospectors didn't see them. They were caught wet-handed and instead of getting beaten gold, they got their bottoms beaten red.

THE BILLY LASELLE in the story lived in the very last house in Cloonabeg. Beyond it there was nothing but heather, cliffs and the sea. It was a house I often visited. During my final years I used to bring Holy Communion to Billy's grandmother on the first Friday of each month, but aside from that I frequently made it the target of a long walk.

I didn't always succeed in the aim, of course. The gossip of the east end diverted me many a time. I might meet up with Peter Lenny in his garden, and that would entail a lecture as long as a book on each leaf of his choice cabbage. Or I might meet Jack Boyce going through Rosnabró, where he lived, and walk would have to yield to talk. But when I did get past Rosnabró, the chummiest village on the island, I always thought, with all the houses shoulder to shoulder and as close as sheep in a pen and got as far as Cloonabeg Strand, then I managed to home in on the target.

A half pint of milk and a half an hour of gab always followed. Very seldom I met Billy's father, Paddy, in the house – a good sign of a fisherman, and he was one of the best – but the womenfolk, his wife and his aged mother, didn't need to be taught how to spell 'welcome'.

The first time I called to Laselles it wasn't hospitality I was looking for but history. Somewhere in the hills or hollows behind their house was the Preesoon, an extermination jail for priests in Cromwell's time. My interested nose couldn't locate it so I made for Laselles to borrow a pair of their eyes.

A footpath curled like a scythe through their meadow with the tip of it at their door. I was quickly made welcome even by the dog, which was a surprise, because Capaill dogs held very narrow views on hospitality. But the same dog had no welcome at all for the chickens who thought that the benevolent atmosphere generated by all the wiping of chairs with cloths, the wiping of hair out of eyes and the wiping of hands in aprons indicated a radical change of climate in the house and a repeal of the Aliens' Act against themselves.

The granny, old Mrs Laselle, sat me down by the window where she audited my face against the accounts she had heard of it and stroked my hand with a blessing far better than any of mine.

Little Rose was there. She was eleven and she had never been to the mainland and knew nothing of mainland ways or mainland animals: she had no idea at all about what kind of sound a goat made.

Her brother, his failure as a gold-digger behind him, was sitting at the fire with the air of a successful contriver about him. He had one shoe off and one shoe on. A rocker 'had fallen' on his big toe and split the nail and shut the school door against him for several days.

It was Vincent, an older brother, who brought me up through the fields, over the scudding gap in the hills and down the other side to the Preesoon. We went through a bog and over a carpet of luck: such a profusion of white heather I had never seen anywhere else.

'I have been here before,' I said to Vincent.

'And you didn't find it,' he said with exclamation marks between each word.

'No,' I admitted, feeling I had dealt a severe blow to the corporate intelligence of the clergy. Even as I said so, the land sat pick-a-back on the shoulders of a cliff looking straight down into the sea.

'There,' said Vincent, pointing at a ravine. 'That's Prees-oon.' If I had been looking for a galleon and he had pointed out a fallen tree to me and said 'There she is' I wouldn't have been as surprised as I was.

When you look for a prison, you look, at the very least, for a building with four walls, constructed of stone blocks, probably grey with small windows. Below me there wasn't a building at all but simply and viciously a natural tunnel through the cliff. To the Cromwellians it was a natural for a prison, designed by God to punish idolaters. It had a roof and two side walls, so the ventilation was a great deal better than in the dungeon near the harbour mouth; a plentiful supply of fresh water because the stream from the bog to the sea flowed right through it; and every chance to escape, either up forty feet of sheer rock into the muskets of the guards or down one hundred feet of sheer cliff into the heaving sea below.

Seventeen priests were imprisoned there at one time or another in the years after 1653. Only one of them survived and he did it with a dive so astonishing for a man crippled with starvation that no teller of boys' stories would invent the like.

It was a French cutter which was passing along the coast that gave him the unpremeditated courage to jump, and what he began prodigiously he finished prodigiously. With strokes devised by desperation he swam out through the creek to the cutter. His guardian angel turned the helms-man's head and the boat hove-to. The French sailors had seen floating corpses before but never a swimming one until then. They lifted him aboard, then resumed their southerly course and five days later all Bordeaux was talking about him.

A number of the families on the island still remembered in their prayers the sixteen who died, but the Laselles didn't pray for them, they prayed to them, and whenever they prayed for something special – a fine day for the hay, a letter from the boy in England, a market for lobster – they got it. 'Holy martyrs of the Preesoon' was how they invoked them;

71

and only those legalist clerics who think that God is spancelled by their own paltry rules would stop them.

There was an occasion during the Land War of the late nineteenth century when curses outnumbered prayers in Laselles' house. At the time they were sheltering a Co. Tipperary man called Hayes who was on the run from the law and to whom that part of the island suggested not prison but a refuge from prison. He was the first man in Ireland to kill a landlord during those troubled times.

His father brought the rent to the landlord but the landlord informed him that it wasn't his face coming up the avenue he wanted to see or the inside of his fist with the money in it but his back and the backs of his sons going east the road for the last time. His mind was on eviction not collection. Young Hayes took the money from his father, put it in his left hand pocket and a pistol in his right. He walked up to the big house and gave the landlord the choice of left or right. The landlord chose suicidally.

Hayes spent seven months in Inish Capaill hiding in Laselles' house and not even the priest knew they had an extra one in the family. The only time he used to go outside was early in the morning before even the rabbits were rambling but it was such a stroll that gave away his secret eventually.

A woman who had been up all night in a neighbour's house watching by a deathbed saw him as she was going home and began to speak of the stranger in the island. Questions asked are like bloodhounds loosed; the police quickly follow. Curses don't help any. The woman kept talking. There was no solution but to run further, and Laselle got him away on a schooner carrying kelp to Glasgow.

FROM LASELLES' HOUSE there was a short-cut home to mine. At the outset it made the heart raise its pace but after it scraped through the gap in the Cloonabeg hills, it took life easy and free-wheeled down into a valley where the Ceatharoo people got their turf and at last, like the Ceatharoo people themselves, it climbed unadventurously to their village.

A man lived in those parts who in my mind connected village and bog as essentially as the road. His name was Dan Haughton. For nine months of the year it was impossible to pass through Ceatharoo hiking it or biking it without seeing Dan or, rather, without being seen by him.

His house was abutting on what the road-signs people call a complex junction. If there had been cars in Capaill, it would have been the place where some unlucky day, at ten past three, Brigette driving her minicar from the school west along, Mick Dunny bringing his turf lorry from the northern bog, Jack Boyce trucking lobsters to the harbour from east in Rosnabró, the postman scorching in his van up O'Farrell's bóithrín, and myself pointing a bonnet at the sky from the steep hill to the south would have all met in the worst collision of noise since Cromwell. Dan's house had in fact the best machine gun position in the whole island but when Dan got you in his sights it wasn't killing was in his mind but parley.

Dan was a great talker and his talking matched his face which had a set prefabricated appearance: he was at his best in prepared pieces, recitations and the like. Indeed the very first time I met him he recited for me.

Brigette had invited me over to her father's house for a rattle of talk and Dan was there visiting when I arrived. They asked him to recite for the priest and he did precisely that, firmly coupling his eyes on to mine and ignoring the rest of the audience although there was a 'come all ye' slant to his piece.

It was in praise of farmers. By upbringing I wasn't very responsive to farmers' propaganda but sitting there with a large bowl – not a cup, mind you, a bowl – of steaming tea in my cupped hands, in front of a noisy fireplace as big as a monk's cell, and seeing Dan as earnest to impress the adjudicator as any ten year old would be at a feis, I concurred entirely in the sentiments he was expressing and when he finished I put a cushion of praise on his chair for him to sit on.

As he was in the beginning, so he remained for the seven

73

years and he saw nothing incongruous in stopping me, for example, on a morning in May and reciting a Christmas greetings poem which had as many stanzas as Christmas used to have days. The stanza addressed to the 'sailors crossing the blue' was particularly memorable because he gestured long and grandly like Columbus on his column in Barcelona while he was saying it!

In an island of big fires Dan kept the biggest and that was why he had to spend the entire summer cutting and footing and spreading turf in his bog in the pit of the valley. During those three months if you wanted to speak to Dan you had to give your shoes a pair of shining soles in order to effect the meeting.

Quite apart from the ticklesome pleasure that Dan's verse-speaking gave, at the end of such bog journeys there was also the chance that I might meet old Carrie Lombard heading home with her donkey and her pale blue umbrella and her knitted red cap, looking like something out of a Himalayan expedition, colourful and shy.

Or, better still, Chris Donnelly might be working in the next trench to Dan putting on a bizarre exhibition of Gaelic football. Donnelly was football mad and every five minutes or so the game he was playing in his mind would overcome him with excitement and he would toss a sod into the air and with a wild shout, 'It's yours, Chris', he would field it like a champion, huggingly, on its way down.

Dan regarded those interruptions as utterly undignified. To him saving the turf was a religious act, which demanded solemnity and silence. He took great pride in the deliberate yet dainty way that he built his reeks: he was the island's finest architect.

Once when I said I would like to take a picture of him standing in front of his cottage, he suggested as an alternative background a reek of his turf. So it was there we went and he stood on the south side of his brown gallarus and he wanted to know if it would be noticed that he wasn't all decked up. The only thing that will ever be noticed about that photograph will be the moulded, the carved set of the rugged island face.

Dan was by no means a young man but he scouted my contention that all that work in the bog made his life a hard one. 'Not at all,' he said. 'I spend the summer getting the makings of a fire and I spend the winter sitting at it. 'Tis a good round life.'

7

Men Put Asunder

IF BRIAN LYNCH HADN'T picked up the bit of wrack on Lacka strand on the morning after a north-easterly gale, there wouldn't have been an argument between himself and his brother, Seán. And if there hadn't been an argument that day about the piece of wood that came in with the tide, the probability is that there wouldn't have been a corpse floating in the water seven months later. Various people, myself included, were blamed in different measure for Thade O'Leary's death but if there was one object more than another that should have been on the coroner's table, that object was the bit of flotsam.

I questioned Brian about it later on and he told me that when he spotted it first, four tumbling waves offshore, he couldn't make up his mind if it was the curl of water which was turning it around and around, or if the object itself was writhing and twisting and eeling and coiling quite independently of what the sea was doing. When, minutes later, he bent down to pick it up at his wet feet, his fingers told him it had the feel of wood, but his mind knew better: it had the sinuous, crimpy shape of a snake.

Brian Lynch was a woodcarver. It was a talent that spurted out of his ancestral veins. His grandfather, Barthy, had made many of the tables that people still gathered at for their Sunday bacon and cabbage, and at every wake in the island at least half the women were sitting on chairs that Barthy put under them. Brian had no formal training in his craft: the chisel and the mallet were his only tutors and the only students he went to art school with were his own fingers.

What he carved mostly were high relief panels of island scenes and island life. In these he rebuilt Cromwell's Castle, and he excitingly stood the beacon on the lifting rocks at the mouth of the harbour like the horn on a rhinoceros' head. Indeed the only time the donkeys got any ease when the turf was being saved was when they rested in Brian's 'Day at the Bog'. He sold his pieces to the tourists, and many were the Lynch donkeys that were tethered to the sides of suitcases and many were the Lynch fishing boats that were moored in duffel bags when the visitors left for the mainland.

But his real preference was for his driftwood creations. While he was working on these, the money-earner stitched up his pockets for days at a time, and the artist lived on his fancies. When a bit of interesting driftwood came ashore he took it as a prompt from God. He felt he was then working alongside God or apprenticed to God as a finisher. His hands took a piece from God's ocean; his eyes put a title on it; and his chisel made the title easier for people to read.

The prompt that he got on the strand at Lacka was this: 'Brian, you are looking at the last snake of Ireland, the good snake that didn't drown when Patrick wheeled it into the sea. It floated away like timber and like timber it has got old and gnarled. Take it home with you and make it young and supple again.'

He carried off the piece of driftwood in his arms. It was nearly five feet in length from end to end. 'No, from tongue to tail,' Brian corrected himself as he turned and twisted the turny-twisty thing first one way and then another. There were two sharp spines protruding from the tip of it: 'I won't have to do anything with the two of ye,' Brian said to them. 'Ye are the forked-tongue.' Then tapping the head with a happy finger he said, 'I'll put the fangs back in your jaw, so I will, and when I do, some hiker will be bitten. It will scare the money out of his pocket.' He laughed at the audacity of his own conceit and confident as a snake charmer he made his way uphill to Fylemore where the Lynch house was situated, close to the great cliff that gave the place its name.

When he arrived at the house Brian rested the wooden snake on the ridge of the half-door and looked in. 'Is that a bit of firing you have?' asked his mother from inside the kitchen where she was seated in a wheelchair, a little to one

77

side of the door.

'Firing! 'Tis not indeed,' he answered as he leaned over to release the bolt. 'The people that will make firing of this, I will make firing of them.'

'Huh. Your threats wouldn't frighten a moth,' Agnes Lynch said coldly, and then with rather more animation she shouted towards the door leading off the kitchen to the parlour, 'You can come out, Miah. It's all right. It's only Brian.'

Miah Lynch was a neurotic. He never went out of doors and as he emerged from the parlour and walked towards a bench seat near the fire, his pasty face witnessed to the fact that neither sun nor wind had coloured it for years and years. The bench seat was his chosen land just as the spot near the half-door where his mother sat in her wheelchair was her regular station. In fact there was a connection between the two because from her strategic position Agnes could hear whenever footsteps would be approaching the house and she would then sound the alarm for Miah who would do an almost vertical take-off from the seat and rush for refuge to the parlour until she would issue the all-clear. And that all-clear was given only if the feet coming up the path proved to be the feet of Brian, of Seán or of Chrissie, Miah's brothers and sister.

Miah had the astonishing idea that if somebody from outside the family saw him face to face, he would drop dead. His mother and Brian and Seán and Chrissie were like the organs of his own body, his eyes and ears and hands and feet and therefore were no threat to his life, but an outsider was like a bullet aimed at his heart. In one sense, even more astonishing than Miah's bizarre notion was the fact that Agnes indulged him: she nursed his crazy idea by keeping watch for the approach of Chrissie's friends and Seán's fishing mates and Brian's customers.

When Agnes called 'It's only Brian', he emerged. He sat at the fire and began looking intently at his hands. By the way in which he held them out in front of him, a person would think he was reading an invisible book. Then he reversed the position so that it was the backs of his hands that were towards his face almost in a gesture of keeping something at a distance. He repeated this ritual several times, finally bringing his hands together before his face as though he were praying, but his thoughts were at no higher level than his wrists.

'Brian,' he prompted.

'Yes, Miah?'

'Come over and look at my hands. They are wasting away.'

Brian crossed the kitchen to have a look.

'Not at all, Miah man,' he said reassuringly. 'They are as big as shovels. They would dig a drain for you.'

While he was saying this, it wasn't at Miah's hands he was looking at all but at the piece of driftwood in his own hands.

'What's that, Brian?'

'It's a snake, that's what it is.'

There was a snort from Mrs Lynch. 'That thing a snake?' she sneered. 'That bit of rotten twisted stick?'

'Twisted, yes. Rotten, no.'

Brian turned around to face her. 'It's alive, this bit of wood is. To me, it's a snake.'

'Well, not to me,' she said. 'I can't see any snake in it.'

'Of course you can't. Your eyes are bounded by Cunnane's wall and J.J.'s reek.'

Brian turned back to face Miah again.

'Can you see it, Miah?' he asked. Then he stretched out his left arm fully and with his right hand he moved the piece of wood menacingly down along that left arm. 'Look, he is gliding silently down a tree in Africa. Can you see it?'

'Yes, sort of, Brian.'

'It won't be "sort of" next week. You will see it as plain as any black man. I'll open the snake's mouth. I'll fill it with vicious teeth. I'll round his belly. I'll make him as smooth as china.'

The mention of china made him think of Chrissie. 'Where's Chrissie?' he asked.

'She said she was going over to Bridie's,' his mother answered and then she added with a sharpness that put an edge on practically everything she said, 'Another giddy goose like herself. Nothing will do her but to be reading love stories. Love stories indeed! What's this island coming to? Reading about people who don't exist and seeing snakes that don't exist. Rotten wood is rotten wood and rotten wood is firing.'

It threw fuel on the fire to mention firing. 'Ah, firing!' Brian shot back at her. 'Can't you think of anything but firing? The way you are talking you'd think that God made trees to boil a kettle!' He put his snake down reverently on the workbench. 'Did you ever hear of rafters, did you, or cradles or coffins or the Cross that Christ died on?'

Miah crossed himself three or four times in a racing hurry to cleanse the air of blasphemy.

'I heard of them, clever man,' Mrs Lynch retorted, 'but apart from the Cross I don't need them. I have rafters over me, and I see no sign that we shall be needing cradle or coffin soon.' Then raising her voice she said, 'The one thing we do need is firing.'

And 'firing' was the word that went down the cliff path to Seán as he came up. Agnes fixed an ear on him. Miah put the palms of his hands on the seat ready for take-off. But it was aborted when she said, 'It's all right, Miah. It's only Seán.'

He came in the door in a rush. He had a face on him the very opposite of Miah's: hard and angular and varnished by weather.

'Did you bring firing?' Mrs Lynch wanted to know.

'Did you bring firing?' Brian mimicked in a flash, his words tripping up the heels of his mother's.

'No, I didn't,' Seán answered.

'But isn't that what you went out for?'

'Yes, but I brought you something instead of it, something better.'

'I don't see you carrying anything,' she said, puzzled.

'I think I know what he means,' Brian said. 'It's firing for the mind, isn't it, Seán? In other words, news.'

'How do you know?'

'Seán, there are times when you remind me of J.J. Tierney, when you look as if your head will crack unless you

80

open your gob.'

'Clever fellow, aren't you? How is it you go on living with stupid people like us?'

'To get all the news, of course.'

'What news, Seán boy?' Agnes cut in on their sharp interchange. 'Is it tasty?'

'It is, indeed.'

'Is it about somebody I know?'

'Yes, it is. Somebody you know very well in fact. I'll give you three guesses.'

'Bridie Mulconry?'

'No, not this time.'

'Fr Kiely?'

'No, not the priest either.'

'Thade O'Leary?'

'The very man,' Seán conceded. 'You're a great guesser. You always get it in three.'

Relishing the compliment, she set herself to guess the ingredients of Seán's sweet pudding.

'He is putting more dry cattle on the common.'

'No.'

'He is taking over from Jack Boyce as ganger.'

'No.'

'He is buying a boat to do out the *Sapphire*.'

'No.'

'Well, it must have something to do with work, if it's about Thade O'Leary.'

'It has nothing at all to do with work.'

'Nothing at all do with work,' she repeated slowly, and looked at Seán to see if she could read the news in his face. He was smiling.

While this dialogue was developing, Brian was leaning over Miah again. He was examining his wrists carefully.

'They are as thick as oars,' Brian said.

'Who are?' Seán asked, taken aback and looking across at Brian.

'Miah's wrists, idiot.'

'My pair are as thick as thieves,' Seán said impishly.

'Your pair of what? Wrists?'

'Lovers, woodpecker. Thade and Chrissie.'

Mrs Lynch butted in. 'Say that again,' she gasped.

'Thade is courting your daughter Chrissie,' said Seán bluntly.

'What!'

'Chrissie is walking out with Thade.'

'Oh, the hussy.'

'How do you mean "hussy"?' Brian objected. 'What's wrong with it?'

'She never told me: that's what's wrong with it.'

'Ah, don't be ridiculous, Mother,' said Brian, differing again. 'She's old enough, goodness knows. It wasn't today or yesterday she learned to wash her face.'

'No, and it wasn't today or yesterday that God said: "Honour your father and your mother".'

'Where is the dishonour for God's sake? She'd have told you if anything definite was decided between them.'

'Definite!' she roared back. 'There's only one thing definite, and that is it will have to stop. He is not coming in here.'

'Well, if he is not coming in here, Chrissie will have to go out, won't she? I mean, if they don't live here, they will have to live there.'

'You shut up. I am the one who decides who is going to live where. And it is my decision that Chrissie lives here with me until I die.' She said this with a menacing tone of finality.

But Brian kept up the argument. 'So that's why you don't want her to get married,' he said. 'You are a selfish old woman.'

'I am not a selfish old woman,' she answered plaintively. 'I am a helpless old woman. When I'm dead she can marry J.J. if she wants to.'

The mention of J.J. gave her an idea. 'J.J. will know if it is true,' she said.

Seán had been quiet for a long time, but now he too got irked with her. 'I told you the truth,' he said. 'I saw them. They were walking out together. What does that mean?'

But no one ever got the better of Mrs Lynch in an argument and she answered, 'You could see a man and a dog walking out together, and what would that mean?'

Then turning to Brian she said, 'Brian, go down to J.J's and tell him to come up: that I want to see him.'

'What good is that half-wit going to do you?' Brian wanted to know.

'He may have only half his wits, but the half he has is worth more than the full amount that others have,' she answered, looking at each of the three sons in turn.

'But, sure, Chrissie will be back soon; she will tell you.'

'Chrissie would deny sunlight if the sun wasn't there to contradict her. Go and do what I tell you.'

With a petulant shrug of his shoulders, Brian left to do her bidding. Seán too stirred himself. He picked up the hatchet in the alcove of the fireplace, and edging Miah aside as he did so he said to him, 'The bloody thing can't even draught with you.' Then he made towards the half-door saying to no one in particular, 'I'll get a bit of firing.'

As he passed the work-bench, he noticed the bit of driftwood where Brian had left it. 'God, there's a grand bit,' he said. He picked it up, muttering, 'He could make nothing out of that, anyhow; it's too twisted.' He turned around to face his mother.

'Could he, Mother?' There was no answer.

In a timid voice Miah said, 'It's a snake.'

'Whaat?'

'It's a snake.'

'Yeh, and I'm a bear,' Seán said sneeringly. He examined the bit of driftwood with a new interest. 'Snake, did you say? Well, it's a dead snake now!' He went out the door, chuckling.

'Mother, did you see what he took?'

'Huh.'

'He took Brian's snake.'

'What do I care? 'Twas only a piece of stick and he can get another piece any tide. The point is: where can I get another Chrissie? Daughters don't float into Lacka after a storm.'

A snatch of a song in the distance put an end to her

83

speech.

'It's J.J.' she said to Miah, who bounded out of his seat, dashed across the kitchen, and hurtled into the parlour, slamming the door behind him.

Two minutes later, J.J. appeared at the half-door with a donkeyish spread of teeth across his face. He entered, and without a greeting to Mrs Lynch, he shuffled all around the kitchen, darting glances here, there and everywhere. He was wearing his customary long coat which enveloped him completely; he looked boneless inside it and you wouldn't even know if he was wearing trousers or not.

'Where is he?' he asked.

'Asleep.'

He tiptoed over to the room door and put his hand behind his ear to scoop up sounds. He shook his head.

'Bedad, he's a fierce light sleeper,' he said. Then he half trotted from the door across to the hearth and he lightly brushed the palm of his right hand across the top of the bench seat. His face brightened. 'He isn't gone to bed very long, Mrs,' he announced.

'What do you mean?'

'I mean his seat is still warm.'

'Don't be stupid, J.J. That's the heat from the fire.'

'Heat from that thing! You could throw a flea in there and it wouldn't even pop. You are telling me fibs.'

'Do you ever tell fibs, J.J.?'

'Me? Never!'

'What do you know about Chrissie and Thade?'

'One is a woman and the other is a man.'

'That's just what I mean. Are they courting?'

'Courting! Is it codding me you are? Sure nothing ever goes courting on Capaill except the seals. I was over there one time in Ooghnaroantee and the like of the antics ...'

'I'm asking you again: are they courting?'

'Course they're not. 'Tis the wrong season now altogether.'

'Listen, J.J. I'm not talking about seals. I'm talking about Chrissie and Thade. Are they walking out?'

'Sure, that's private sort of work, Mrs. How would I

know?'

'You're not the man you were, J.J. 'Tis the first time you were ever second with anything. Seán knows it and you don't. Seán of all people. If the Board of Works anchored a new island in the bay he wouldn't see it.'

J.J. was hurt. 'Well, maybe I do know something but I'm not going to tell you.'

'Why not?'

'Because I was told not to, that's why.'

Mrs Lynch knew she had turned his flank. 'Tell me, J.J,' she said bringing up reinforcements, 'who gives you the big candle for the window at Christmas?'

'Yourself, of course. Who else?'

'And who puts the seat back in your pants when you have ripped it?'

"Tis you have the bold hand with the needle, Mrs.'

'Would you like a biscuit, J.J?'

'There's nothing I'd like better in the whole munching world.'

'They're in the tin in the dresser.'

J.J. hurried over to the dresser, took down the biscuit tin and was just about to lift off the lid, when Agnes said, 'Put it back again. I have changed my mind. You wouldn't tell me the news.'

'I'll tell you. I'll tell you. How many biscuits will you give me?'

'Six.'

J.J's fist plunged into the tin and emerged with the trophies. With his mouth full of biscuit, he strolled back to her wheelchair.

'Well? Tell me.'

'Chrissie and Thade are walking out all right.'

'Is it going on long?'

'The first time I saw them I was abroad on Inish Leopard at the turf. So 'tis three months anyhow. There was a big strand the same evening and they came down to where the roilleachs were feeding and she was leaning on him.'

'Oh! Oh! And did you see them since?'

'I'd say if you were to give me a biscuit for every time I

85

saw them since, you would have to give me another half dozen.'

'You ruffian; go on, take them.'

J.J. paid a return visit to the biscuit tin.

'Do you think they will get married?'

''Tis as sure as rain. They are tearing for it, I'd say.'

Then like something that would happen in a play, there was a scrape at the door and Chrissie entered. She took off her coat and gave herself a playful smile in the mirror.

'You are looking pleased with yourself,' her mother observed. 'Had ye a good chat?'

'We had, faith.'

'What did ye talk about?'

'Oh, this and that.'

'Did you say this and did he say that or were ye in agreement?' Agnes asked cuttingly.

Chrissie rounded on J.J. and savaged him with a look.

''Twasn't I told on you, Chrissie; 'twas Seán.'

'The stupid fool!'

'You didn't answer my question, Chrissie.' Mrs Lynch was nothing if not persistent.

'We were in agreement, if you want to know.'

'Ye were, were ye? About what?'

'That, number one, we are suited to each other and number two, we are going to get married.'

'I see,' said her mother, never a woman to be bested in a set-to. 'Well, you forgot to mention number three and number four. Number three is time and number four is me. Time will tell if ye are suited to each other and I'll say if ye are going to get married.'

Chrissie didn't back away from her. 'How do you mean you'll say if we are going to get married? What have you got to do with it?'

'I am your mother. That's what I've got to do with it. You can't get married without my permission.'

Chrissie's temper flared. 'Permission, my foot!' she said. 'That thing left the country with the coffin ships. I don't need your permission. I am over twenty-one. In fact, I'm nearly thirty-one. I'm not a baby, you know, or your slave either.'

Her rage silenced her mother for the moment, and sensing that she now enjoyed a slight advantage, she changed her tone of voice to something much more conciliatory and she asked, 'What have you against Thade, anyhow?'

'I have nothing against Thade. I don't blame him for wanting to marry. I blame you. You are the only daughter I have and you are going to let me rot here in this house.'

'That's nonsense. I'm not going to leave you. Thade knows that I have to look after you. We have been talking about all of this. After we are married, he will live here with us.'

'Oh, will he now? Did he ever hear it is manners to wait to be asked? And he is not going to be asked. I made a promise to Miah and I am going to keep it.'

'A promise? What sort of promise?'

'That nobody comes in here to live because if he does Miah will die.'

'You don't mean to tell me that Miah is going to drop dead if some outsider sees him? Such trash.'

J.J. was standing between the two of them, following their words with magnetised interest. Brian came in but he paid no heed to him.

'I know it is trash,' Mrs Lynch said, 'and you know it is trash. But Miah doesn't. He has this fear and fear can kill. Thade stays out.'

And as she said that, Seán came in with a few bits of timber clamped to his chest. 'Clear the way there for the donkey,' he said flippantly.

'Donkey is right,' Chrissie snapped. 'Stupid ass, you couldn't keep it to yourself. You had to bray about it.'

Seán took a few strides in the direction of the fire. As he did so, Brian gave a sharp look at the timber he was carrying; then he looked across to his bench. The snake was missing.

'Hey,' he roared. 'Where did you get that wood?'

'On your bench. Why? Did you want it?'

'That was my snake.'

'Oh, a snake was it?'

'You hacked it to pieces. You killed it.'

87

'Yeh, but don't you know snakes are dangerous?'

Brian charged across the kitchen, his head down, and butted Seán in the chest. Seán staggered back and the wood fell on the floor. Then, with his arms free and arms flailing, he hit back mercilessly. Much taller and much stronger than Brian, Seán drove him across the kitchen, landing punch after punch.

There were shrieks from Chrissie and 'Stop it! Stop it, Seán!' from Mrs Lynch. J.J. was hopping with excitement. One final pulverising punch to the side of the head sent Brian sprawling against his bench. He tottered to the floor.

J.J. swept to the door and rushed outside roaring, 'A fight in Lynchs! A fight in Lynchs!'

Seán went back to where the wood fell out of his arms. He collected it and piece by piece he slammed it on the fire.

THERE WERE PEOPLE on the island later on – I freely admit it, there were many people – who said that I shouldn't have married Thade and Chrissie at all. They argued that I was too inexperienced to size up the situation at Fylemore. I was three years younger than Chrissie, they said, and eleven years younger than Thade, and they implied that not even God Himself could put an old man's head on a young priest's shoulders. I daresay there was a lot of truth in what they said. Maybe if I had blessed holy water at ten more Easters, if I knew without stepping back from the crib in which direction I should be pointing the faces of Caspar, Melchior and Balthasar at Christmas time, if the page edges of my Breviary had turned from gilt to smoky brown, I might have seen Mrs Lynch's intransigence, Seán's bitterness, Miah's neurosis and Brian's artistic flightiness in a clearer light.

But it is easy to fight a battle all over again and bring about a different result, when one has read the history books, and as things stood it wasn't on any other door in the island, it was on mine that Thade and Chrissie knocked to ask to be married. Besides, when you are young you see castles in Spain rather than cottages in Capaill; you give marks for what is right rather than red strokes for what is wrong; you expend just one cigarette on your misgivings.

In any case, everything was in order according to the text books so who was I to add to the prescripts of canon law? Every island off the west coast bore the marks of inter-marriage as well as glaciation, but as bad luck and good genetics would have it, Thade and Chrissie were only in the thirty-first cousin category. They hadn't been married before. Thade had never been a monk in Mellaray and Chrissie had never taken the veil. Neither of them had been off the island for more than two days at a time so there was no question of letters of freedom. When I consulted the baptismal register their names jumped off the page to assure me that they were valid candidates for the sacrament of marriage. And far from being under pressure from any source to get married, the opposite was the case. There was a general canon which stated that all who are not prohibited by law can get married: Thade and Chrissie were not prohibited by any law and therefore they had a perfect right to get married.

'First of all, you get the rules right; then you go on to see if the couple are right for each other'; that is what the professor, later a Cardinal, used to tell us in Maynooth. I got the rules right in this case and as far as I could see Chrissie and Thade were right for each other. Chrissie had a great heart: she had put up with Miah's tantrums for years; she had tolerated Brian's untidy bench in her tidy kitchen because it was the only place where he had enough light to work; she had resigned herself to Seán's obtuseness because if it weren't for his lobster pots there wouldn't have been anything in the cooking pots for any of them; and she had done every hand's turn for her arthritic mother who showed very little affection to her in return. Indeed the only service she didn't do for Agnes was something she hadn't the physical strength to do and that was left to Seán who, all credit to him, rolled his mother up to Preesoon in her wheelchair to say her prayers for the sixteen priests any day when the sun was clear and the sod was firm.

If Chrissie was known for her kindness at home, Thade

was known for his energy everywhere. He had cows on the common, sheep on the Glasillaun, and a currach in the water. He had burn marks on every finger from hauling in heavy fish. When the mushrooms started showing their heads he was out before priest or gannet every morning; all that anybody else could find in the fields were his tracks on the dew. If you wanted a fresh mackerel, Thade was the man to go to: his mackerel were as fresh as the rain. And he was famous for his Pinks and Queens: if you blew on them they would collapse, they were that floury.

With Chrissie's heart and Thade's head, they were sure to succeed and I put no obstacle in their way between my door and the Lord's altar. The one feature I was doubtful about was the private ceremony they requested; Chrissie seemed to think that the quietest way of doing it was the best, so she arranged for a wedding at which there would be only five of us present: Chrissie herself, Thade, Bridie Mulconry as bridesmaid, Stevie Ward as bestman and myself. I advised her to tell her mother but she wouldn't hear of it. I offered to break the news to Agnes myself, but she vetoed that too. She was convinced that if her mother knew of her intentions beforehand, she would find a way of stopping her going to the church, even if it meant pitching herself out of her wheelchair at the very church door. Whereas, if the ceremony took place unknown to her she couldn't get Seán to roll her over to the church to scratch the writing out of the register. I had my doubts, but I gave way on them; I asked myself how could I who only met the woman every First Friday know her better than her daughter who was with her for every chime that the clock made.

In between our meeting and the marriage, the plan was that, whenever Seán and his mother would be out, Brian would go to work on Miah to try to soften his attitude towards Thade. Brian used the womanly technique of routeing the argument through his stomach and he fed him the spring lamb, the summer spuds, the autumn mushrooms and the winter mackerel from Thade's supply store. Brian used to tell Chrissie that a bit of Miah's wall was falling every fine day, so when the day fixed for the wedding was approaching my only real fear was that the day might be wet and there might not be any pilgrimage to the Preesoon.

As things turned out, it was a grand sunny day and I felt that God Himself had become part of our conspiracy, but even in a little plot like ours the unexpected can happen and the unexpected did happen in the shape of a butter-box. If I had been the oldest and wisest priest in western Christendom I couldn't have anticipated gunpowder in a butter box.

It was Chrissie herself who inadvertently left the time-bomb lying about. When Seán set off with his mother for the prayers, Chrissie and Bridie who were in hiding behind the bounds wall south of the house waiting for this moment, left their place of concealment and moved somewhat erratically towards the house. Their uneven motion was due to the fact that they were carrying a loaded butter box between them. Hanging limply over the top of the box there was a parcel of good quality brown paper. Bridie was clearly dressed for an important occasion in costume and hat; Chrissie's trousseau was in the brown paper parcel.

When they got to the house there was a great scamper. Chrissie took hold of the parcel and went upstairs to put on her finery and Brian who was on sentry-go and who had hustled Miah to his oubliette, took out the contents of the butter box and along with Bridie stacked them away in the cupboard: an iced cake and spiced beef and tomatoes and a bottle of whiskey and bottles of stout and a tin of biscuits and a box of chocolates and bananas and a box of dates shaped like a race track with painted Arabs running all over it.

Chrissie didn't spend much more time dressing herself than a child would and in a jiffy she came tripping downstairs in a cascade of happy laughter from Brian and Bridie. Brian said the outfit was like varnish he would put on teak: it made a lovely thing lovelier and Bridie in a more down-to-earth phrase said that Thade would pass out when he saw it. Then with a crack about how they should keep an eye on the priest so that he wouldn't tie a crooked knot, Brian sent them on their way to my house.

If they were to keep an eye on me, I in turn was keeping

an eye out for them. And I was able to do it without having Aggie 's all-seeing eyes on the back of my neck because I had got her out of the house earlier by giving her a half day off to go home to her sister's place in Ceatharoo. Thade and Stevie were already with me, and strangely all I can remember now about the time while we were waiting for the two girls is the shine on the men's boots: they were like mirrors that you could part your hair in. I wonder now if I had my head bent, if I was apprehensive, if that's why I saw so much of the boots. Eventually, Chrissie and Bridie arrived: I had the door open for them before they put a toe on the steps, and then, when the road east and west had no life on it except maybe a black beetle, the five of us went down to the church.

Nowadays we have a separate tome for each of the sacraments, and for the life of me I can't see that the liturgical library we now carry around with us in our cars has made the slightest difference to the baptised, confirmed, absolved, married or anointed, but in those days we had all the formulae from the baptising of infants to the blessing of boats in one little book that you could slip into your jacket. So I found page 216 in the *Collectio Rituum* and I began: 'In the name of the Father and of the Son and of the Holy Spirit, Amen. Dear children of God, you are come today to seal your love for each other before God and in the presence of these witnesses.' Then after reading an address on the origin, the purpose, the holiness, the blessings and the responsibilities of marriage, I turned to Thade and I asked him; 'Thade O'Leary, do you freely and willingly take Chrissie Lynch here present as your lawful wife according to the laws of God and of Holy Church?'

He answered, 'I do.'

I then focused my attention on Chrissie and I asked her; 'Chrissie Lynch, do you freely and willingly take Thade O'Leary here present as your lawful husband according to the laws of God and of Holy Church?'

She answered, 'I do.'

Then I said, 'Now that you are united in holy matrimony, join your right hands' – which they did with a bit of steering from myself – 'and say: "I, Thade O'Leary take you

Chrissie Lynch as my lawful wife to have and to hold from this day forward, for better for worse, for richer for poorer, in sickness and in health till death do us part".'

I shiver now when I think of it, but on that day when the words about death were being recited, who could have foreseen a dripping coffin navigating its way up the aisle parting all the women of the island on one side of the church from all the men on the other side?

Then Chrissie said her piece: 'I, Chrissie Lynch, take you Thade O'Leary as my lawful husband to have and to hold from this day forward, for better for worse, for richer for poorer, in sickness and in health till death do us part.'

Next I said my little bit in Latin: *'Ego coniungo vos in matrimonium in nomine Patris et Filii et Spiritus Sancti. Amen'*, and in the most solemn tone that I could produce I declaimed, 'I call upon all of you here present to be witnesses of this holy union: What God has joined together, let no man put asunder.'

What none of us in the church knew was that at that very same moment in Fylemore things were being put asunder.

When Seán and his mother came home from their outing to Preesoon, both of them immediately noticed the butter box on the kitchen floor. Agnes was more interested in who brought the box than in the box itself. She questioned both Brian and Miah on where it came from. Brian lyingly denied all knowledge of it saying he was out along the rocks looking for a snake not a butter box; and all that Miah could tell her was that he had heard Chrissie's voice and Bridie's voice in the kitchen, and Chrissie's step on the stairs.

'One or other of them must have brought the box, so,' Agnes concluded.

'Whoever brought it,' said Seán, 'it is a grand box and I am claiming it.'

'Who said it was yours?' Brian demanded.

The fight was on.

'I didn't say it was. I say it is,' was Seán's answer. He caught it, turned it upside down and sat on it. 'I'm sitting on it,' he proclaimed, 'so, it's mine. Squatter's rights. A squatter

93

has to be pushed off, you know.' He said that with a challenge to Brian's eye. 'It will be grand for fishing from the rocks, just what I wanted for ages.' He tightened his hands in a clench, one above the other as he would if they were holding a rod and he raised and lowered the imaginary rod a few times. 'Can't you see me,' he continued, 'on the top of Doonmore on a summer's day with my feet on the ground and my bottom off it? Ah, the comfort.' He tapped the side of it, appraisingly. 'Sound bit of timber in it,' he said. 'I'll give it a slap of creosote. It will last while there's a fish swimming' – a remark which put him in mind of his pots and he left, saying he would be out seeing after them for an hour or so.

Seán's departure gave Brian his chance. He went across to where the box was squatting and he said, to no one in particular 'There are two ways of looking at a box: Seán's way, it's a stool, but this way' – and he turned it right-side up – 'it's just a big hole, and big holes are dangerous.' He went to the fireplace; he picked up the hatchet without letting his mother see what he was doing; he placed it silently in the box and moved with it towards the half-door. 'I suppose none of ye want this piece of furniture in here,' he said as he left.

A minute later there was the sound of timber being split outside in the yard. 'Mother of God! Did he take the hatchet, Miah?' Agnes asked and then reversing the wheelchair to the half-door she called, 'Brian, Brian! You're not breaking the box?'

'What box?' he called back. 'Stool, do you mean?' There was another squeal of splintering timber. The battle lines were drawn.

WHEN I WAS going to secondary school I learned the couplet:

> Great wits are sure to madness near allied
> And thin partitions do their bounds divide.

Our teacher, Fr Jim Kelly, explained to us that the people

whom Dryden had in mind were the great geniuses. Now I wouldn't go so far as to claim that J.J. Tierney was a great genius but, to employ a phrase often used on the island, he was 'a bit of a genius'. I didn't know anybody else in Inish Capaill in my time who could startle you with words in the way he could. When, for example, he assessed the heat of Lynchs' fire by saying you could throw a flea onto it and the flea wouldn't even pop, or when he told Agnes that there was nothing he liked better than biscuits in the whole *munching* world, what was that but a touch of genius?

He had a genius also for collecting information: given changed circumstances and a change of clothing he could have been an investigative journalist. He knew everything that was going on. He had the birds of the air in his eyes and his ears had scoops like shovels. If a young man on Capaill had an erotic dream about a young lady, it was J.J. who would wake up! And when I thought on the day of the wedding that there was no life anywhere east or west the road except a black beetle, I was very badly mistaken: J.J. had the five of us under observation. And as soon as we entered the church he went haring off to Fylemore to bring them the latest bulletin.

That was one side of the thin partition in J.J; on the other side there was a definite kink, and subsequently I was never able to understand how intelligent people like the Lynchs went along with his crazy suggestion that they should have a referendum on Thade and Chrissie.

But first things first. J.J. burst in through Lynchs' door shouting, 'Mrs, I have news. Big news. The biggest news I ever brought you. 'Tis a wonder I haven't gumboils from holding it in my mouth.'

'Well, spit it out, so.'

'I saw people going to a wedding, five people.'

'Five people: that's not much of a wedding,' she said dismissively.

'Ah, but wait till you hear who they were, Mrs.'

'Tell me.'

He positioned himself near the dresser. 'Five names: five biscuits,' he traded.

'J.J. you would turn the Bible into biscuits if you had the chance. Go on, take them.'

His right hand dug into the biscuit tin for his bribes and then he paid them out from his right hand to his left hand saying as he counted them, 'One, a biscuit for Fr Kiely and he'd need it; there's not a pick on him. Two, a biscuit for Stevie Ward; he can bring it home to the children. Three, a biscuit for Bridie Mulconry; she can put it ahide in her new handbag. Four. Are you listening to me, Mrs? Four, a biscuit for Thade O'Leary, but his mouth is too dry to eat it now, I'd say. And five, a biscuit for whom do you think? ... Chrissie Lynch.'

'Chrissie Lynch?'

'That's what I said.'

'You're fooling me!'

'I'm not fooling you. I saw them. Going into the church, the five of them. The priest leading. Then Thade and Chrissie shoulder to shoulder. And Stevie and Bridie like a rearguard. And they were all dressed up, I'm telling you.'

'Dressed up for what?' To ask a question such as that meant she was floundering.

'Dressed up for a wedding. What else?'

Seán appeared at the half-door.

''Twas God sent you,' she said. 'J.J. here has a story, and I don't know what to make out of it.'

Seán wasn't interested in J.J's story but in his box which was missing.

'Where's my box?' he demanded. At that moment Agnes couldn't have cared about the alienation of an entire creamery, let alone one butter box.

'Ah, it's all right,' she lied, 'Brian took it out to the shed.' And with that she gave J.J. the floor. 'Tell him what you saw, J.J.,' she prompted.

'See, Seán,' J.J. began, 'I was up in the priest's field kneeling behind the wild cabbage stalks, when who did I see coming in the priest's gate only Thade O'Leary and Stevie Ward. 'Twasn't bound for the Reek they were, I can tell you; they were dressed real smart. "'Gor," I says to myself, "there's something on here." Up with them to the priest's door, but before they could put a paw near the paint, wasn't it opened in front of them! "Ah, ha," says I, "the priest is expecting them".'

He was glorying in his role of uninterrupted narrator. He continued, 'That was queer enough but a short while afterwards, didn't Chrissie and Bridie come in the gate as well and up to the door with them, and they were dressed something grand. Handbags, gloves, the lot. And do you know what? The door was opened for the pair of them, too, before the new shoes ever got near the mat. A couple of minutes later the four of them came out and Fr Kiely as well and down with the whole troop to the church. They weren't chatting much: they were sort of solemn. There was something big on their minds, I could see. It wasn't a decade of the Rosary they were going into the church for, that's for sure.'

Agnes looked up at Seán from her wheelchair. 'What does it mean, Seán?'

It was J.J. who answered, 'I told you what it means: Chrissie and Thade are getting married.'

'Do you think it is true, Seán?'

'I suppose it could be. They are fierce thick, you know that.'

'But I stopped her, didn't I?'

'You said stop but you can't say stop to a train.'

And then something happened that stopped the rolling talk dead in its tracks. Brian came in the half-door and his arms were full of timber. It was neatly stacked, piece upon piece upon piece, like large volumes that a library assistant would be carrying. He made straight across the kitchen to Seán.

'I thought you might be looking for this,' he said to him jauntily, standing quite close. 'Your fishing stool. I didn't like it the way it was. It was very common-looking, really, so I have made some alterations and what I have here for you now is much better. It is what they call a "do-it-yourself" kit. All you have to do is to put these pieces together and you will have not a stool but a chair. There's the seat,' and he threw down one of the sides of the butter box; 'there's the back,' and he flung down another; 'and there are the four legs,' and he spilled four laths of unequal size, which in their earlier existence had been the bottom of the butter-box, on to the floor at Seán's feet. 'Oh, and you have spares as well, a spare seat and a spare back' and displaying the final two broken sides of the butter-box, he tossed them noisily on top of the rest.

Seán was so flabbergasted, he was so immobilised by what was happening to him that he listened mute, like a well-coached actor right to the very end of Brian's sarcastic instructions. Then the final clatter of timber on timber roused him and he made a drive for his brother but Brian wasn't going to make the same mistake that he made on the day his snake was killed and he scampered out the door.

Seán didn't follow him outside. Instead, he leaned against the jamb of the door, pursuing him with blazing eyes and a cold threat: 'The next time you set your heart on something,' he hissed, 'I'll wrench it away from you.'

'I hope you don't mean me, Seán,' said Bridie Mulconry suddenly appearing from the other direction. He moved aside and she entered the kitchen.

'Hello, Mrs,' she said, a trifle nervously, nodding to Agnes. 'There's two people outside and they would like to come in. Will I call them?'

'Do, Bridie, do. Who are they?'

'It's a surprise. They are a new pair on the island.' Bridie stepped back towards the door and called, 'Come on in,' and as Chrissie and Thade filled the frame of the door with a picture that horrified Mrs Lynch, Bridie announced 'Mr and Mrs O'Leary.'

Chrissie advanced towards her mother. Thade stayed at the door. He stretched a hesitant hand to Seán but Seán ignored it.

'Mother, say we are welcome.'

'You are welcome as my daughter, not as anything else,' she answered coldly and added, 'He isn't welcome at all.'

'But he is my husband now,' Chrissie pleaded.

'Not in my eyes, he's not.'

Thade, a big man who could have disentangled a heavy

98

sodden net with ease, but not an indoors situation like this, advanced awkwardly a few feet.

'Stay where you are, Thade Leary.' She dropped the 'O'; it was the same thing as dropping a bomb.

'I only want to say I'm sorry for the way this happened,' Thade explained. 'The priest said it would be all right.'

'The priest should stick to playing with his cats. He isn't as good at playing with people.'

Chrissie came to my defence. 'Mother, what are you saying? It wasn't his idea. We asked him to marry us.'

'Me you should have asked.'

'I wanted to, but you would have said no.'

'Yes and I still say no. I say no to you; I say no to the priest; I say no to the marriage.'

Brian came in and he put a steadying hand on Thade's back. 'It's all right, Thade boy, hold tough. She'll soften out.'

Not she. 'I'll soften when my joints soften,' she spat. And wheeling her chair in Thade's direction as if it were an armoured car, she sprayed him with vicious words. 'Let me tell you something, Mr Leary' – the 'Mr' was the equivalent of Christ's 'heathen and publican' – 'you won't add my slate house to your cottage and your currach and your sheep and your cows. Not six foot by two of a bed will you get in this house. So get out. You're not wanted.'

That was too much for Brian. 'Ah, for God's sake,' he protested, 'stop talking like Queen Maeve. You'd think the place was a bloody mansion.'

'Big or small, it's mine,' she spat back at him.

'Yours!' Brian roared. 'How is it yours? It's ours. It's the family house. It belongs to the five of us.'

That was the cue that J.J. needed in order to get back into the drama, and he took it. 'I know what ye'll do,' he said positioning himself in the middle of the kitchen as if it were the centre of a stage. 'Take a vote on it. Five voices. Five votes.'

'Good idea,' Brian said, impulsive as ever. 'My vote goes to Thade.'

'One for, none against,' said J.J.

Mrs Lynch quickly cancelled out Thade's advantage.

'I'm voting no,' she said.

'One for, one against,' J.J. announced.

'Chrissie, you're next.'

Chrissie went over to where Thade was standing and she gave him a squeeze of the elbow. She looked up at him and she said, 'Thade is welcome in my house.'

'Two to one. Thade leading.'

J.J. had never umpired a game in his life and he was enjoying his new role down to his toes.

It was Seán's turn to vote. He wasted no time about it. He said a blunt 'no'.

Simultaneously, Chrissie and Brian asked 'Why?'

He aimed his answer at Brian. 'What you're for,' he said 'I'm against. What you like, I smash. What I like, you smash. What you will, I won't. I warned you, didn't I? "The next thing you set your heart on," I said, "I'll wrench it away from you." This is it.'

'But you are voting for or against Brian,' Chrissie put in. 'The vote is for or against Thade. Thade never did anything against you.'

'My mother never did anything against me either.'

'Good boy, Seán,' Agnes said.

J.J. was hopping with excitement. 'It's a draw at two all,' he announced. 'That leaves it up to Miah. He has the casting vote.'

Everybody at once looked towards the room and the locked door. Brian was the first to make a move in that direction and then Chrissie and then J.J. and then Bridie.

'Miah, were you listening?' Brian asked. 'Do you know what's going on?'

'Yes,' came the feeble answer from behind the door.

'Say another yes, Miah, please,' Chrissie pleaded. 'Say yes to Thade. He is no stranger. He is my husband now. He is your brother-in-law. He is one of the family; he won't hurt you. Say yes, Miah, say yes.'

'Do Miah, do, boy,' said Brian supporting her. 'Remember what I told you. Mushrooms with a wrapper of dew; mackerel that haven't stiffened; spuds like a ball of white wool. Man dear, say yes to the spuds.'

Agnes summoned Seán and he wheeled her to the room door so now they were all there, Chrissie, Bridie, Brian, J.J, Seán and Agnes; all except Thade who was still standing, a lonely and bemused figure, just inside the half-door.

'Miah, listen to me,' his mother said in the strongest, most riveting voice of them all. 'Do you want to live or die? – that's the question.'

'That's *not* the question. That's not fair,' Chrissie exploded. 'You said yourself all that was trash.'

'Live or die, Miah, live or die?' Agnes persisted.

'Live, Mother, live,' Miah answered, half shouting, half sobbing.

'Do you want Thade in or not?'

They all held their breath. The answer was very low and indistinct but it wasn't yes.

'Out loud, man, so they can hear you,' his mother roared, pressurising him.

'No!'

'That's it, so,' said J.J. 'The final score: three to two. Thade loses.'

Thade turned away. Chrissie followed him to the swing of the half-door. 'Don't worry, Thade,' she said, 'you didn't marry them or their old slate house. Wait for me at the end of the path. I'll pack a case. I won't be five minutes.'

A great deal happened in those five minutes. Brian left to stand shoulder to shoulder with Thade and to wait for Chrissie where Thade was waiting for her. Bridie made a fierce attack on Mrs Lynch saying that even the savages in Africa would sit down to a meal and have an old song or two, and show a bit of love when a daughter would get married. A selfish bitch, she called her at the end of her harangue and got thrown out. 'Oh, you are good at throwing people out,' Bridie said spiritedly as she left. J.J. also was ordered off the premises but he didn't mind; he had enough gossip gathered to last him a month. And even Seán, who said he would make up a fire for her – 'you are trembling,' he commented – was motioned out of the house. So she was alone and pitiable and calm and scheming and unassailable on her choice of battlefield when Chrissie came downstairs with her suitcase.

The act of packing had somehow weakened Chrissie's resolve. She looked vulnerable, and her mother sensed it. Agnes adopted a wheedling tone: 'Come over to me, Chrissie girl.' Chrissie dropped to her knees near the wheelchair so their eyes were on one level, looking closely at each other. Chrissie's battle was already lost. Every pass she tried, her mother parried.

'Why are you so cruel to me on my wedding day?' she asked.

'It is you who are cruel to me on your wedding day,' was the answer.

'A man shall leave father and mother and cleave to his wife,' Chrissie quoted.

'Yes, but where does it say a woman shall leave her crippled mother and cleave to her husband?' was the brilliant counter.

And having won the intellectual argument, she couldn't fail in her emotional assault.

'What is going to happen when I call, "Chrissie, I want you" and you are not there? To find my beads. To light the lamp. To pull the curtains. To boil the kettle. To dress me. To feed me. To give me a smile. The boys don't know how to smile, Chrissie; did you know that? Did you?'

'No,' said Chrissie in a weak voice, reeling.

'There's lots of things you don't know: how a mother suffers and what a gain a daughter is, and how useless sons are. Miah and his fears, Seán and his pots, Brian and his bits of wood. Don't leave me to them. Please. I beg you.'

The battle was over. Mrs Lynch called off the attack. 'Tell him you can't live with him for the present. Ye will have years together later on' was how she phrased the terms of surrender.

Chrissie rose from her knees and walked slowly to the door. At that very moment Brian returned.

'What's keeping you?' he asked.

'I was talking,' she answered.

He went to lift the suitcase. 'No, Brian,' she said, 'leave it.'

'Aren't you taking the case?'

'No.'

'Aren't you going with Thade?'

'No.'

'But why? You said you were going.'

'Leave me alone. Oh leave me alone,' she said and ran out the door crying.

Brian faced his mother. 'This is your doing,' he rasped. 'It is the devil's doing. What God has joined together, you have put asunder.'

TIME TOOK A LEAP of six months but Chrissie didn't leap with them. She continued to live at home, mistress of the chores but of nothing else. Her heart was in another place, but her hands were tied to her mother. At every opportunity she froze Seán out of the kitchen but it was poor compensation for the other freezing process that was immobilising her relationship with Thade. What had happened was that a killing frost had attacked the potato stalks as soon as they put their heads above ground and now the whole field of love was blackening.

Unlike Chrissie, Thade *did* take a leap with the six months but it was a leap in a direction no one ever expected him to take, a leap into a pit of *sughlach*. He sensed that everyone in the island was mocking him and he could hear their sniggers in the very sounds of the tide among the rocks, and their derision in the chuckle of the wind. His currach got smashed up and his spade broke out in a sort of measles. So he jumped from bow to bar and from field to foolishness. Pat O's pub became his new commonage, and it was a sort of alcoholic beef broth that he was drinking there, day after day, as he lowered animal after animal down his gullet.

He wouldn't listen to reason from Chrissie, from Brian, from me, or from anybody. His pain was his only advisor; it was the ignominy of the situation that alone had a steering hand at his elbow. It was as if he was being driven by a fierce gale and he couldn't bring the boat head to wind to take in sail.

Everyone said it couldn't last, but no one expected it would end as quickly or as terribly as it did. What *was* expected, however, *did* happen: the beginning of the end was staged in Pat O's pub. Thade went on a huge batter. As he downed drink after drink, he left so many rings on the counter in front of him that it looked like linkwire. Every now and then, as he finished a glass, he smashed it on the floor. With all the glass around, the pub took on the appearance of a road after a hard frost settled on top of thawed snow. Pat O couldn't stop him and nobody else dared because he said he would make glass splinters of the chin of the man who tried.

After months of hard drinking, Thade's drunken state didn't make news anymore in Lynchs' house but it *was* the making of news on this occasion and as usual it was J.J, the man of all knowledge, who ran to Fylemore with it.

They were all at home when he got there: Mrs Lynch and Chrissie and Brian and Seán in the kitchen and Miah securely in his refuge after the pounding that J.J. gave the cliff path.

Without any sort of greeting or beating about mannerly bushes, he flung the news at them. 'Thade is drinking oceans,' he said.

'Oceans of what?' Brian asked.

'Courage,' J.J. answered.

'Courage?' Brian's puzzlement spoke for them all.

'Yes,' said J.J. 'Pat O pours it out of a whiskey bottle and says "Another jorum of courage for your belly, Thade". And when that is gone and the glass smashed, he says, "Give me another glass of courage, Pat O, and when I have courage enough I'll go up to Lynchs"'.

They were alarmed, all of them, and Chrissie most of all. For the first time in six months she turned to Seán for help. 'Do something, Seán,' she pleaded. 'Stop him. He mustn't come in. I don't want to see him like this.'

'Brian, put the bolt on the door,' Seán directed and it was a sure sign of something terrible to follow that Brian did his brother's bidding. That sort of unprecedented family

104

unity was how you timed the first tremor of an earthquake. Brian slammed-to the top of the half-door and bolted it. Seán then dragged the heavy kitchen table and jammed it into a barricading position up against the door. And then he and Brian took up sentry stations at the window.

'Where are yeer guns?' J.J. wanted to know, reading the situation as if it were a Wild West script. At any other time, Mrs Lynch would have castigated him for his idiotic notion, but her only response on this occasion was to pray aloud, 'Sacred Heart, protect us now,' which was asking a bit much of God when she was herself the molten fault that caused the earthquake.

Everything went quiet after that for a spell until a raucous voice could be heard approaching closer and closer, singing the definitive pub song of the island: –

When I was a young man and hearty
I fought and I drank with the best
And I gatecrashed the toffs' garden party
Where I plucked the sweet flower of the west.

Brian and Seán watched him as he came up level with the house. He wasn't on his beam-ends by any means but his lee-rail was definitely under. However, if his limbs were soused, his brain was remarkably clear. 'I want my flower, d'ye hear, before she withers,' he shouted.

He approached the door. 'Shut, is it?' he boomed. 'Well, knock and it shall be opened,' and suiting the action to the word he banged so hard with his two fists together that flakes of paint splintered off the inside of the door. But the besieged didn't open up. 'Right,' he roared again, 'ye asked for it.' He walked away from the door in as straight a line as he could make, for about six paces; then standing sideways on, with his hands locked low in front of him, his knees flexed and his right shoulder bent, he propelled himself violently at the door. The timber squealed at the shock of it, and the table, although Brian and Seán were buttressed against it, gave way an inch.

'Let him in, for God's sake,' said Brian, 'or do ye want to

take a vote on this too?'

Thade came to the window. It was clear from his expression that he was focusing his eyes too high to see anybody but the ultimatum was well directed. 'If ye don't I'll get the crowbar to your precious slates,' and with that he made for the outhouse.

She was outflanked and she knew it. 'Open up, Seán,' Mrs Lynch directed. Seán pulled back the table and Brian released the bolt. Thade looked over his shoulder and wheeled. He kicked the door open and lurched into the kitchen. His right arm was stretched out fully in front of him to clout the doorkeeper but when he saw that it was Brian he looped it around his shoulder instead.

'Wisha, how are you, Brian boy?'

'Grand, Thade. How's yourself?'

'Middling, only.'

J.J. sidled up to him. 'My dear friend, J.J, how are you? I'll suffocate you in biscuits yet,' and with that he looped another arm around J.J.

'Come over to the table, Thade, and sit down,' Chrissie said gently.

'I will then, Chrissie, as it is you who asked me.'

He walked to the table, half carrying the pair and half being steered by them and he sat down. Chrissie had a cup and a saucer and plate there almost as soon as he was there himself.

'What will you have?' she asked.

'Tea and the wedding cake,' he answered.

'But that was six months ago, Thade.'

'I don't care. I want some of my own wedding cake. I got none of it.'

'All right, Thade boy, just a minute. Is there anything else you would like?'

'There is. I'll ask you to come home with me when I'm finished.'

The hard combative voice of Mrs Lynch re-opened hostilities. 'She will do no such thing,' she said.

Thade turned his back on the table to face her. 'Why not?' he asked.

'Because you are a drunkard, that's why.'

Thade rose unsteadily to his feet and slouched towards her.

'You are a drunkard, too, for that matter, only you are drunk with meanness.'

'Thade, Thade,' Chrissie said soothingly. But it was no use. Thade kept walking until he reached the wheelchair and leaned down menacingly over Agnes, with his big hands resting on the arms of the chair.

Brian tried to pull him away by the sleeve. 'Thade, calm down, boy,' he said.

'I won't till I say what I came to say,' he answered and he elbowed him aside. Then looking straight down at the stony face beneath him he said his say. 'Mrs Lynch,' he began and he wiped his mouth with the back of his hand as if her very name were slobber, 'there's something I want to tell you. You remind me of a conch shell that the sea would throw up. You're twisted and you're hard and there's nothing inside in you only a cold bleak heart. You smashed my marriage and you smashed me and so help me, I'll smash you.'

He whacked the arm of the chair for emphasis. The sound of it roused Seán into action. 'Leave her alone, you lout,' he roared and he came up from behind and drew a vicious kick on Thade. Thade turned and in spite of his unsteady footing, he pulled Seán into him with his left arm and he crossed an almighty right to his chin. Seán went down in a crumpled heap.

Thade turned to Chrissie and in an amazingly quiet voice he asked, 'Will you come with me now, Chrissie? There's no one to stop us. Come on before 'tis too late.'

'I can't, Thade,' she said.

He was dumbfounded. 'Can't! Is it you don't want to?'

'I do, Thade, I do, I do. But I can't. Can't you see I can't. Look at this shambles of a family. How can I?'

'All right then, Chrissie,' he said sadly. 'I won't ask you anymore.'

He turned away from her and went out the door slowly and quietly. He pulled the half-door into position after him, looking back one last time at Chrissie. And then the hard slap of the air on his face, or else the hurt of finding himself expelled from the house, not by the ballot of his enemies but by the decree of his wife, must have chafed his passion afresh because suddenly he began to shout the words that were so quiet before – 'Not anymore, I said, not anymore.'

He half ran, half stumbled down the cliff path yelling as he went, 'Lynchs. Liars. Liars. Lynchs,' and then there was a long harrowing desperate shriek. And after that, silence.

Brian ran to the door. 'Chrissie! He's over the cliff!' he cried.

'Oh God. No. Oh, no!' she screamed.

Brian ran across the yard and down the path. J.J. followed him shouting, 'Thade! Thade!'

Seán merely picked himself up and felt his jaw.

Mrs Lynch, still cowed in her wheelchair, made no move whatsoever.

Chrissie dragged herself to the table and sat on the chair where Thade had been sitting. She picked up the cup he was going to drink out of, looked vacantly at it, and crooked her finger through the handle. 'Oh, Thade, Thade,' she whispered and lowered her face slowly down on the table.

Miah opened the door of the parlour and peered out.

'Is he gone, Mother?' he asked.

'Yes, he's gone,' she answered.

'He won't be back, will he?' he asked.

'No, he won't be back,' she answered.

8

God's Good Skipper

JAMESY PRENDEVILLE CONCEDED that Jack Boyce was a good man to tell a story but always maintained that he himself had a better lip for it.

Hear Jamesy telling his story of the scapular and the fish:

'I was fourteen when it happened. 'Twas St Martin's Day, the eleventh of November. My father and myself left Capaill at one o'clock. We had our own hooker and we were bound for Westport.

'My father was a very good-living man, God rest him. He'd rather sail without a rudder than without a Rosary beads. He was a good hand always at fingering the Rosary: all the way up along the coast he used to stage out the journey by saying decades of the Rosary here and there. In one place the intention would be that we'd duck the shoulder of an ebb tide; in another that the wind would go more south and give us a push from behind, and there wasn't an island or a head where the hooker didn't scatter holy water on the bones of drowned men and dead men.

'I had no Rosary beads of my own at that time but I had a brown scapular with a picture of Our Lady on it around my neck.

'Well, as I say, we left Capaill at one o'clock. We were going for a cargo that day so we had no fishing gear of any kind with us. 'Twas just the kind of weather you'd expect in November with all the holy souls about, sort of shadowy, the purgatory time of the year.

'When we started there was a good thick mist, not like a shutter altogether, more like a dark curtain on the sea's window. But about four o'clock the shutter went up, and 'twas so bad we couldn't see what was holding up the sail. I went up for'ard and for eight hours I didn't see my father and he didn't see me.

'"We'd better anchor, Jamesy," said my father. We were close to the southern side of Clare Island so we edged our way inshore. I was taking the soundings up for'ard and I need hardly tell you we hadn't one of those fancy plummets aboard that yachtsmen have. I was using the anchor chain for the job. If an islandman was put to it he'd plough with a scythe. We're used to making do with what we have for what we haven't.

'Anyhow, before I heaved the chain overboard the first time I took off my brown scapular and hitched it to a link of the chain two fathoms up from the bottom so that I'd know when 'twas getting right dangerous.

'"Twas for things like that my father always said I was the cutest of the whole family and he'd rather have me in the boat with him than a man his own age. "An ounce of brain is better than a ton of muscle," he used to say. The most of the men in my time could hoist a sail faster than me but there was none of them who usen't to watch if I was plaiting a reef in mine. I'm not saying now I was good at school or anything like that. In fact I hated school. It's just that myself and the sea got on together like two fish in a shoal. What I liked always was the laugh of the water when a boat kissed it.

'We let go the anchor in six fathoms and there we stayed just outside the noise of Clare Island for eight hours, hoping we'd get the sight of our eyes back and praying the same two decades of the Rosary, the Resurrection and the Ascension, over and over, the Resurrection because 'twas full of light, don't you know, and the Ascension because of the way Our Lord lifted up and that's what we wanted the fog to do.

'Midnight came and a new day and the fog cleared. It didn't gather itself up into the air as we expected; it moved away from us on all sides in a wide circle. My father became a shape again and the sea gave a big stretch and the island shore gave an explanation for all the racket that was going on.

'I pulled up the anchor and we got under way. We had Clare for company for a while and then we worked out into

110

open water again. Clew Bay was dead ahead of us and with the wind from the west all we had to do was to shake out the sheets and we'd reach Westport as sure as a toy with a square rig.

'But, blow me, the fog was playing a children's game with us and the circle soon closed in around us again.

'"What'll we do now, Jamesy?" asked my father, though 'twas really impatience that was asking the question.

'"The same as before, father. Listen for an island and anchor in the lee of it."

'Clew Bay, the inner part of it anyhow, is packed with islands. They're like the biscuits in those tins you get for Christmas, with the curly paper all around them. How could we miss?

'But miss we did. We were back in a world of nose and ears. I knew my father was smoking his pipe but I couldn't see it. I was up for'ard all ears for an island, all hands on the chain but not a breaker could I hear or a bottom feel. We were lost.

'How could you get lost in your own back garden, you might say. Only if you were blindfolded, as we were. We had no compass; a compass cost three years' rent. Going to Westport we simply navigated from point to point and even when we were away out at sea fishing we came home by watching where the sun was going or where the gulls were going.

'What was after happening us (but, of course, we didn't know it at the time) was that the wind had backed from west to south and so we were sailing north towards Achill when we thought we were moving east up Clew Bay. Two hours or maybe three and nothing happened, and then, as unexpected as thunder there was a sudden thump of a breaker right ahead of us.

'"What'll we do, Jamesy, what'll we do?" my father shouted and whenever he said the same thing twice at sea, he was scared.

'"Gybe her, gybe her!" I roared and the mainsail came across with such a crack you'd think we had ten teachers aboard. Praise be to the Mother of God, we came safe out of

111

it, but now we felt more lost than ever. There was no breaker like that in Clew Bay.

'Shortly afterwards we heard the low chatter of an island and I sounded our way inshore with the chain and we went to anchor again. We were there six or seven hours swinging on the chain.

"Twas eight o'clock when the first bit of light squeezed through, and a bit of the island followed it through the gap and then as often happened with a blown up fog 'twas as if someone stuck a pin in it and all of a sudden only rags of it were left. The sun came out and we were looking at an island that could have only one name for its shape and that name was Achill Beg. We were as far north-west of Westport as we were south-west of it twenty-one hours before.

'There was no use talking about fairies or blinking our eyes hard and hoping that Achill Beg would change its shape. There was nothing for it but more work and a hard beat to Westport. But not before we said a prayer to the best pilot there ever was, the Blessed Virgin Mary. The two of us got down on our knees and we thanked her for looking after us with her Rosary and scapular.

'Then, still on my knees on the foredeck, I began to pull up the anchor. You won't believe this, but if my father was alive he could tell you the same thing: when I got to the scapular two fathoms from the end of the chain wasn't there a pollock, a six pound pollock, caught on it? Never before and never after did I see the like of it.

'I was mad at my father afterwards when he gave it away to Miss Marron in Westport. I wanted to keep it and bring it back to Capaill but he wouldn't hear of it. "What good will one stale pollock do in Capaill?" he argued. "We're not going to spend another night on the sea tonight and 'twill be stale by the time we get back tomorrow."

'So Miss Marron got the pollock. I wouldn't begrudge her a long hundred of them any other time because she always gave me a stand and "She sells us salt and oatmeal cheaper than anybody else in Westport", my father added.

'"All the same 'tis Our Lady's fish, father, and 'tisn't right for anybody to eat it." No good for me to argue the

112

point. I was standing on the wharf at Westport and I was only fourteen, and out of the boat my father regarded my fourteen as fourteen and no more than fourteen.

'We went up the town with the fish.'

I THINK I WAS probably the only person in Inish Capaill who called Jamesy 'Jamesy'. Everybody else, including his sister Peg who was married to Mortimer O'Farrell called him 'Skipper'. He was responsible for the rechristening himself, but not out of arrogance, rather out of innocence.

It happened in Westport about ten years after the pollock episode. Jamesy was there with the hooker for a cargo of salt. One advantage the sailor's son has over the farmer's son is that the sailor hands over the boat while the son is still a young man: the driving seas hustle him into making his decision. But the land is an old man's ally and it doesn't rise up in strength like the wind to tell him that a young man would fight it better. So at an age when farmers' sons couldn't set fire to a furze bush without being told, Jamesy was standing at the tiller of his own boat, masterful in eye and hand.

Two things bring men into a pub: content and discontent. Jamesy was as contented as a goldfish; the hooker was loaded and the tide would help at eight in the morning so in with him to a pub. 'Twas mostly sailoring men were drinking there, and among the number a shoal of herringmen from Capaill.

There was one man standing at the bar by himself; clearly an Englishman isolated by the local gossip. There was only one thing Jamesy liked better than the lift of the sea under his stern and that was talking to strangers so over with him straight to the man at the bar. He was English, it was true, but a rum or two took the edge off nationality and in ten minutes their heads were close enough for them to ask questions out of interest and not out of mere curiosity.

'What do the strips on your sleeve say?' Jamesy asked him. 'That's a language we don't go in for here.'

'It means I have a skipper's rank. You might have noticed a freighter called *British Monarch* tied up at the Deepwater Quay. Well, I'm the skipper of her.'

'And I'm a skipper, too,' said Jamesy. 'My boat is called *Morning Star.*' The Capaillers heard him saying it and when they went back home they brought with them something far more exciting than the good price for their herrings, a mocking story. A gale of laughter swept the island and the damage it left behind was a new nickname: 'Skipper'.

But as the gales and years drove past, it ceased to be a joke and became like one of the nicknames of history – the Conqueror, the Just, the Builder of Cities – a fact. Jamesy could fight a storm better than any man who might have his coat all silked with decorations. When the Atlantic roughed up, there wasn't a boat that wouldn't play duckling to Jamesy's duck. He could measure wind as well as a gull's wing; he knew better than mackerel where the drag of the currents were; and in his head the seafloor rose and sloped. He was everything that the old Dutch meant when they said a man was a 'schipper' and the Dutch weren't given to flattery.

When I arrived in Capaill, Skipper Jamesy had long since given up standing in the stern of a hooker and had taken to sitting in the most unusual chair in the island.

For anybody interested in having one like it, here is the formula: – fetch yourself a pre-Steel Age timber porter barrel; knock out the flat top and put aside for later use; remove the upper hoops: now borrow a saw, gauge the diameter of the barrel and cut right down along the diameter to about the mid-section. When you get that far, turn it over on its side; buy a saw because the man who gave you the first one won't lend you another and cut in along the equatorial line of the barrel until you meet the vertical cut. When you do, a sizable piece of wood, arch-shaped will come away. And what you have left is the low curved front and the high curved back of your chair. Insert the flat top in the mid-section as a seat, get out your varnish brushes, shine up the remaining hoops and you have a barrel chair after the style of Jamesy Prendeville.

From the chair Jamesy presided over the comings and goings of his two farming brothers, and superintended the sale of flour : the four or five sacks inside the door were the last links with the old days when the *Morning Star* was a freighter and Prendeville's house was a general stores.

From the chair also, he appraised the progress of the bastibles on the hearth. His most important function every day was to build the fire and to bake the cake for himself, his brothers and his dog appropriately, called 'Sailor'. In terms of weight the cake took a lot of watching because it was as big as the wheel of a mini-car.

Indeed, according to the Skipper himself, it was a full-time job. Every Friday without exception he delayed calling for his old age pension until twenty-nine minutes past six and once when Mrs Daly remonstrated with him for waiting until the very last minute, he told her, 'Well, I just can't come any earlier because I'm busy the whole day watching the cake and I have to say my Angelus at six o'clock.'

When I said that baking the cake was Jamesy's most important function every day, I should have inserted the adjective 'domestic' before 'function' because, clearly, his most important unqualified activity was saying his prayers.

Every evening after his supper he spent an hour or more in the church praying before the Blessed Sacrament, making the Stations of the Cross as slowly as if he were carrying the Cross himself, paying his compliments to the statues of St Joseph and St Patrick and standing rapt as a lighthouse in front of the stained glass window of Our Lady, Star of the Sea.

'Why do you spend so much time in the church?' somebody asked him once. 'Because Our Lord likes to have me talking to him,' he answered simply. Sometimes his gestures were rather demonstrative as when he was discovered in the Crib one Christmas flat out in the straw, lips at the Infant's feet and showing the hesitant kings how they ought really to adore, but his prayers were invariably silent. 'Those women who pray out loud are only insulting God,' he asserted. 'They make out He's deaf.'

Like his father before him, Jamesy was a great hand at

115

fingering the Rosary and he believed not only in building up a reserve of grace for himself in heaven but also in stocking up plentiful supplies of Rosary beads on earth. Not a priest or a nun visited the island whom Jamesy didn't 'conjure by the bowels of misericord' to send him a Rosary beads, and like a devout miser, he watched the holy hoard grow with immense satisfaction.

The joy a new Rosary beads brought to him matched the pleasure a schoolboy feels when he acquires a rare coin or a new stamp for his collection. Contrariwise, one of the most disappointing experiences he ever had was when the postman handed him a little packet from the United States marked 'religious object' but when he opened it the beads were all running around the wee box like a game in a Christmas stocking and even when he had restored them to their requisite sobriety he had the makings of only four and a half decades.

Lighting candles at the shrine of Our Lady of Perpetual Succour was another religious act that he highly prized but he always maintained that the clergy put too high a price on their candles. When the number of candles burnt and pennies collected didn't tally, I concluded that Jamesy had privately introduced bargain prices. This was not a rash judgment on my part because once when I was on my holidays he told my replacement 'I'm fond of Fr Kiely but, do you know, he charges a shocking price for candles. I wonder does he ever think that he is depriving the Mother of God of her earthly glory. There should be no charge at all, in fact. It is the shining light Our Lady wants, not the pennies.' On winter evenings, especially, he hated to leave Our Lady on her own in the dark and I often arrived to find a platoon of stiff young candles standing brightly in front of her. As this was in the nature of a public act of veneration, Jamesy didn't see why private money should pay for it!

The climax of his evening devotions was reached when he left the church and trudged across the churchyard to the grotto of Our Lady of Lourdes. There, with his eyes raised to the blue Lady in the rock, and, after I showed him a picture of pilgrims at Lourdes, with his arms outstretched in Mosaic intercession, he stayed for a quarter of an hour even if the kind of Pyrenean rain, that Bernadette froze in, was falling. There was no grotto in all the Marian world like the Capaill grotto, according to the Skipper: how could there be when he himself transported its two statues of the Lady and the girl in his hooker from Westport?

Praying well doesn't necessarily mean having one's petitions granted but there was at least one occasion when the Skipper's prayers were, he claimed, notably effectual. This was on a Friday in August when his niece, her husband and their three children were due to go back to America.

It was a despatch day for the mail so the *Sapphire* was scheduled to leave the quay around nine o'clock. Once the Yanks got to Killeggan an average speed of even twenty miles an hour would take them with a few comfortable hours to spare to Shannon where they were to board a jet en route from Rome to New York.

But their plans were caught up in a sudden storm out of the night and blown to tatters. The morning was a full brother to the night with heavy lumps of wind and sharp thongs of rain. The wind was from the one point that kept Paddy Mallon sitting at the hob, south-east.

The harbour was in a fit: its mouth was frothing, and the Yanks were fit to be tied themselves. 'We wouldn't get as far as the beacon,' Paddy told them when they asked him if he intended to sail. Everything – wind-force, wind-direction, sea-state and Paddy's reluctance to look them straight in the eye – indicated that the storm had wiped that date off their tickets.

At ten o'clock the husband was at Paddy's door again. 'Is it any better now?' he asked.

Paddy never even looked at the sea. Sailors are like doctors; they have ways of knowing other than by sight. 'No, it isn't,' he answered.

'Well, will it be any better in an hour's time, or at twelve or at one? When do we know for sure?' The Yank was turning imponderables into figures and a man into a computer. He was, in addition, understandably piqued.

'Everything depends on what happens at the change of

117

tide,' Paddy answered. 'The wind might change then or it might calm down or the sea might flatten a bit.'

As a man of the sea, Jamesy concurred with Paddy's assessment of the position but as a man of faith he couldn't agree that the elements would have things all their own way if Our Lord could be got to take an interest in the situation. What happened on the Sea of Galilee could happen between Capaill and Killeggan. The only difference between then and now was that the gale off Gerasa was a north-westerly. The Master was lying nice and handy and the apostles shook Him up and they said, 'Is it that You don't care? Hurry, we need Your help.' And He rose up and He checked the wind and He said to the sea, 'Peace, be still'. And the wind dropped and there was a great calm.

Jamesy was used to talking to the One Who was obeyed by the winds and the sea, but like the apostles he hated to disturb Him. However, the need was urgent now, so in with him to the church where he lit a candle – and paid the asking price for it, a penny! – and said to the Master, 'I'm sure You feel sorry for my niece, Cathleen. Come on, like a good Man; she needs Your help.'

It's not for me to speculate on cause and effect, to determine if the wind just fell at the change of tide or if it was tossed down, to say if the troubled waters simply calmed of themselves or if a Hand running with the oil of heaven touched them.

What is certain is that at one o'clock, Miley in his seaboots called into the post office for the mailbag and people came rivuleting with the water down the boreens, and flowed together to the beach to see the Yanks off. When the waving was over and the *Sapphire* was under way Jamesy returned to the church. 'It's only plain manners to say thanks,' he told me as he went in the door.

And if a miracle, why not a vision? A theological training leaves one somewhat incredulous about such things. Is it because priests don't have visions themselves that they pour sour grapejuice over other people's apparitions? Whether or not, the matter of fact way in which Jamesy recounted his own vision softened a good many of the sceptical lines on my face.

This is how he told it: – 'It was in the church it happened, September twelve years about twenty to nine in the evening. No, 'twasn't a bit dusky in the church because 'twas the kind of day that stores up a pile of light in the sky and gives it out *flúirseach* later on.

'I was going the rounds of the Stations of the Cross and I was just after reaching the eleventh station when I saw, out of the corner of my eye, a figure standing at the foot of the altar. I say out of the corner of my eye because I was giving all my attention to that bully of a soldier – I'd say he was a blacksmith before he joined the army – with his mallet raised above Our Lord's left hand.

'Going from the eleventh to the twelfth station I had a much better look at the figure. I didn't see his face but I'd say he was about thirty years of age to judge by the thickness of his neck. He was wearing a kind of cloak. 'Twas just like the cape for Benediction but it didn't have any of those goldy streaks on the back of it. I was as calm as if I was out fishing on a flat sea. That's what I find so strange now looking back at it. I knelt down for the twelfth station and I prayed it the best I ever prayed.

'The figure was still there when I was walking to the thirteenth station but he was after moving up to the altar. I can't tell you what he was doing. I didn't stare at him or anything like that. I didn't want to disrespect what I was at, following Our Lord up the hill of Calvary. But, when I had Christ's body taken down from the Cross and I was carrying it to the tomb, the figure was gone.

'Should I have given him more notice, I wonder? I do hope I'll see the vision again sometime. I can't tell you how happy I felt.'

Very few of the islanders put any credence in Jamesy's vision and what I regarded as persuasive matter-of-factness they castigated as specious pretence. Maybe, it was a case of the prophet not getting honour in his own country; if the definition of a prophet is 'a man apart who speaks to God', then Jamesy qualified for the title at both ends of the definition.

The bizarreness of the man came out clearly when his brother Peter was dying. Peter was the closest to him in age and in his affections and he in his turn had always admired Jamesy whether as the boy who was wearing trousers while he himself was still in a flannel dress or as the man who made the tiller a magnet for fish while he himself was merely readying the nets.

They had had many adventures together. As boys they had shared a stolen currach in which they had rowed the nine miles to Killeggan, competed in a two mile race which they won and, without even landing for a lemonade for fear the menfolk from Capaill would lift them out of it by the seat of their pants, struck back again across the tumble of the sea to the island.

As grown men they had fetched together from Westport in the *Morning Star* and had fished together in the *Mermaid*, and once when they had the net down, a school of sunfish – as plentiful as the flowers on the wallpaper, Jamesy told me – came rushing towards them from the west, and instead of rolling past decided to do their home exercises around the *Mermaid*; neither Peter nor himself liked one bit of them: they liked them even less when a huge sunfish rose up his full height in the air right next to the boat and nearly harpooned himself on the mast as he flipped over. He blundered into their net and they had to cut it away between curses and prayers.

Jamesy as head of the bachelor family slept in dignified solitariness in the big bedroom; his brothers, Peter among them, slept in three cramped beds in a much smaller room. In an island where the rights of primogeniture were well established nobody saw the slightest thing amiss in this arrangement but when Peter got a disease of the bones and they began to crack like sticks of chalk, the neighbours told Jamesy that he should move him into the big bedroom.

Jamesy refused. He had his reasons. 'Peter wants to go to sleep forever where he always went to sleep. He wants to die among his work.' This latter was a reference to the fact that Peter's fourposter was draped in a fishing net. 'Besides, changing him now will only confuse him and I suppose ye know that at the end of a man's life his mind must be clear in order to fix up his account. The next change of scenery that Peter wants is the sight of God and Our Lady and his own fisherman saint in heaven and not just pictures of them in my room. Anyhow, a man doesn't die in a room, a man dies in a bed and Peter's bed, poor man, looks bigger and bigger now day by day.'

Jamesy was really very fond of Peter and who is to say that in his own eccentric way he wasn't holding the right end of the medicine spoon, but the neighbours supposed that prestige was ousting love so when the Skipper was berthed in the church one night, they transferred the sick man, bed, bedding, fishing net and all into the big room, removing Jamesy's bed from the smiling circle of his dozen protecting saints and relegating it to the infidel bareness of the other room.

Peter died and that left Jamesy in control of the situation again. The wake was held in *his* room so he was the master of ceremonies. As a result they were almost as long as in the last days of Holy Week. The Rosary which opened the first session will be remembered on Capaill for as long as Rosary beads nestle in people's pockets.

'Ye're no good at saying it,' Jamesy told the assembly. 'Ye have no practice. I'm at it all the time, I'll say it.' He did, and with trimmings it took an hour and five minutes.

JAMESY VISITED ME frequently but never as late as Jack Boyce and seldom during the winter. It wasn't I who imposed the curfew on him, it was my homemade gaslight which irritated his eyes and made him weep with vexation. Years of bright sun on broken water 'had melted the outer layers of his eyes' and now only candlelight was friendly to him.

Maybe it was because he was a sailoring man and Jack was not, but what Jamesy said and did during a visit followed a fairly regular course whereas Jack's direction could not be plotted at all. When Jamesy came in for a session of talk he made for my big old-fashioned armchair and relaxed full length in it. As his shoulders dug deeper into the back of the chair, his elbows slid out along the arm-rests and pushed the coverings before them. Not till the brocades rested on the floor did Jamesy rest in the chair.

The next part of the proceedings was to light the pipe. He always had some trouble clearing it for action. When I was watching him, his efforts were invariably mannerly and unavailing; but if I turned away he got it free in a drastic instant. When I offered him a box of matches – Jamesy 'saved' matches the way a child 'saves' sweets – he said 'trés bon'.

O yes, in the Skipper's cascade of talk there were several spatters of French. He had had dealings with their trawlermen and lobstermen on numerous occasions, and once he towed a drifting French boat into Capaill. She had three hundred crayfish aboard 'but the Frenchman had a completely different name for them, *langoustes* or something'. That was a great tow: 'twas worth a good few draws of cognac. 'We turned Napoleon upside down, we had him standing on his hat before we were finished with him.'

For his 'bite of supper' with me, he liked tea, sandwiches, sweet cake and biscuits. Especially biscuits. 'I love biscuits,' he often said. This protestation of love was unnecessary for anyone who was present to watch his hand grapple on them in the tin and lift them out four at a time! Once, he spilled a full cup of tea all over his legs but he shook off the brew and my sympathy in a moment. 'I'm used to being wet, Father,' he said and held out his cup for a refill.

For the most part I kept him on the sea and out of the church while he was with me but occasionally he got the better of my wishes and recited a prayerbook prayer out loud so that I could judge whether Our Lady would approve the sentiments or not. When this happened, he used to take off his cap – something the hot tea or the purring turf couldn't induce him to do – join his hands for the start of the prayer and sweep into the grandiose phrases so different from, so much less meaningful than, his own strong, simple, image-sharp talk. Halfway through, imitating the public prayer of the Church, he used to stretch out his hands in the gesture a priest uses during Mass, hold them steady as his

122

beloved branch candlesticks and at the quiet conclusion he would join his hands again and slap his cap on his head.

I preferred him on sails than on saints. I loved the visit when his mouth filled with the names of boats like the *Irish Girl* or the *John Wesley* or the *Pretty Polly*.

The *Irish Girl* was the first big craft he ever sailed on: Amis was her Master's name and he could squeeze music out of a melodeon as easily as another man could squeeze juice out of a grape.

When others mentioned the *John Wesley* they spoke of timber, pointed to chairs, window frames and sheds, and their eyes got a French-polishing in the process; but when Jamesy spoke of it his eyes took on the same vacant sadness which they did when he recalled his brother Peter; the ship too was a seaman's brother and had died a long hard death on the bed of the Tanees at the harbour entrance.

The *Pretty Polly* was a great lass to bring home baskets of fish and to carry out kegs of rum to the German U-Boats during the First World War. One summer morning when she was going out for fish and not with rum – there wasn't a hump of a submarine to be seen anywhere on the horizon at the time – old Commander Edwards, who got his eye in for shooting during the Boer War and got shot himself later on by the Boys in Ballinasloe, put his submarine chaser after her and blew her out of the water without so much as a first wide shot. 'Wars ruin everything,' Jamesy said. 'The fire lit by the first one isn't quenched yet.'

As a spinner of sea-stuff Jamesy was at least as good as Jack was at exhuming men from the graveyard of the past. He readily admitted that he couldn't hold a shrine candle to Jack when the subject turned to nature study but for all that he had fondled a cuckoo in his hands once and Jack had to be content with loving the bird at a shouting distance.

It was a Sunday morning in the lightness of spring and Jamesy was early on the road to Mass. At Dooneen, just west of the church, he came across the slatey bird hunched on the ground and with the heave of the ocean in its exhausted body. He picked it up, cradled it in his warm hands and brought it through the churchyard to a ledge in the grotto where he left it in the care of the Mother of all living things and the Mother of healing.

During Mass Jack Boyce never said a single prayer because the bird kept cuckooing at every hand's turn of the priest, but Jamesy 'prayed great' because he felt that himself and the Mother of God had put their hands very close together. At the end of Mass when the people came out, the cuckoo flew up to the valley and so it was Jamesy and not the bird who became the centre of attention.

PRIESTS ARE OFTEN on the move, being transferred many times in the course of their work from parish to parish. Each time they change residence they jettison part of their former lives. Furniture, curios, books, even friends are discarded. One picture that has rested for safety on the back seat of my car on all such occasions and that will hang on any wall I'll ever own is a picture of Jamesy that I took before I left the island.

'You'll have to pose for a photo for me, Jamesy,' I said.

'I will of course and welcome, Father,' he answered, 'but I'll have to change my coat first.'

He emerged not in a better jacket but in a more distinctly Jamesian one, the lapel of which went on celebrating Patrick's Day three months after everybody else had torn up their paper harps and which had an archipelago of medals shining down the blue front .

He leaned towards me across the wall of his little garden, his fingers laced together like a piece of spliced rope on a fishing smack. He faced the camera with the set of a man who had looked everything in life straight in the eye.

In my picture you can see the lift of intelligence in the forehead, the curve of artistry about the mouth, the aristocracy of the supplanted chiefs of Ireland in his long nose. The old man appears in the grey moustache and the boy in the gleam of the eyes.

9

Goodbyes

ON A WEDNESDAY AFTERNOON late in July, an expected hour after the mailboat had arrived, an expected knock livened the door. 'Come in, Batt,' I called. It was the postman.

He put a letter down on the table next to me. It was in the Bishop's disciplined handwriting. Without benefit of slitting fingers I knew what it contained. 'Thank you, Batt,' I said with a courtesy that was quite empty for the first time in seven years, one week and five days. He steered the postbag back over his hip and left.

I opened the letter. This is what it said: –

Bishop's House,
Tirella.

Dear Fr Kiely,

I hereby terminate your appointment at Inish Capaill and I appoint you instead curate of Leenog with effect on and from Wednesday next. Your successor in the island will be Fr Newman whom I have instructed to take up residence on Friday of this week. You will be good enough to introduce him to the people and the work and explain to him what his various duties will be. Asking God to bless you in Leenog and wishing you every happiness there.

I remain,
Yours very sincerely in Christ,

† Thomas Murtagh

I went down the narrow passageway to the kitchen. 'Aggie,' I said, 'I'm just after getting a letter from the Bishop.'

'Oooh,' she said, the first 'O' big with wonderment and the others like two small eyes close together questioning me.

'I'll be leaving Capaill next week and going to Leenog.'

'Oooh,' she said again, and in case I couldn't interpret the falling inflexion which she gave it on this occasion, she added 'I'm sorry, Father, and very sorry.'

'Not half as sorry as I am, Aggie.'

I returned to my sitting-room and for the first time that day I was fully conscious of how filthy a day it was. The fog was so low that if there were surveyors on the island they couldn't map anything higher than a hundred feet. The sea was just a narrow grey belt, quite unimpressive. The panes of glass in the window were crying. Ever since that day I am inclined to the view that poetic fallacy is by no means fallacious.

I looked at my paperbacks and wondered how in the name of Pan I was going to scatter in a week what I had gathered in seven years. Then I took down the *Irish Catholic Directory* to see who was Parish Priest in Leenog. Oh, no! of all people, Connolly, who wouldn't have allowed the eleven apostles into his parish before the election of Matthias in case they were a soccer team.

Aggie came in. 'Father, I'm going over to Raymond's for milk,' she said. I could have reached for my squat Bible and sworn on it that she had been to Raymond's for milk not two hours before. The real purpose of the trip was to carry a kind of cream and not to fetch more milk: that I knew. But all I said was 'All right, Aggie, I'll be here in case anybody calls.'

Inside an hour, four people called: Mrs Nally who didn't often leave her throne to walk in the democratic day; Brigette, on holidays from school; her father, Mortimer, who normally called only once a year, a week or so before the twenty-fifth of September to have a Mass said on the feast of St Finbarr on behalf of the saint's cousins, the O'Farrells; and Mrs Dan Ree who always took an interest in church affairs because her front door was the main clearing mark indicated on the pilot charts for the Bishop's Rock. All four lived along the road west between my place and Raymond's so clearly Aggie's milk errand was having social repercussions.

It was a safe bet that, before Batt brought the last of the day's mail to Cloonabeg, the news in the Bishop's letter would have reached there before him.

ON THURSDAY MORNING I rang up Kathy O'Hally in Killeggan to get a salmon for me even if she had to put on her long-legged swimming costume and wade into the pool under the Garda Barracks in Clifden to poach one, and to put it fair and fresh into the hands of the new priest before he boarded the *Sapphire* next day.

On Thursday evening I broke new ground (and the kids broke three glasses, a table lamp, the chain of the W.C. and Aggie's heart) when I had all the children of the island into the house for a party. What they enjoyed best, although it wasn't meant as a part of the entertainment, was the bonfire I built and lit in the failed lettuce patch. I have never got such co-operation in any burn-your-rubbish drive as I did on that occasion.

My worry ever since, however, is that in addition to bringing to the flames armfuls of old newspapers and shirts so patched they wouldn't do now even for patching and Maynooth class-notes that took seven years to compile and that I never even dusted in the seven years that followed and miscellaneous junk that I hadn't either worn, read or used since I was ordained, my worry is that the children may have been somewhat previous in emptying a chest of drawers in my bedroom and so perhaps destroyed the last wills and testaments of people who had a perch of bog or an acre of mountain to leave after them.

ON FRIDAY AFTERNOON Fr Newman arrived on the mailboat. An uplands man, he was unlucky in his first crossing and he got a few tails of the cat across the shoulders from a punishing sea.

'Now you're an islander. You have been baptised,' I said to him, as I gave him a hand out of the punt.

'It's quiet,' he remarked as he walked up the pebbly beach watched only by a six-footer rock just above the high-water mark that I had christened the Harbour Master. What he meant by 'quiet', I knew, was: the islanders don't give one much of a welcome, do they?

I don't go in much for quotations from the clergy but

one was clearly necessary at this point, one from the 'Friday Sayings of Fr Blake'.

'Look, John,' I said, 'don't think because there is nobody at the boat to welcome you that you are unwelcome. It's just that they don't know how to deal with two priests at the same time. They think that if they come out in strength to greet you it will seem like rushing me away. Everything in right order: first tears, then smiles; the old priest first, the young priest afterwards.'

Only the first impressions were wrong. In the course of the evening Aggie fussed over his damp coat, Jamesy came in with an assurance of scorching weather for the next two months, and I gave him a half rick of dry turf, a self-servicing Raleigh bicycle and a battery radio that was so good on the trawler band he would never get lonely for talk.

I consulted the 'Friday Sayings' on two further occasions during the run of the evening. The first was when he asked me what course of Instructions was prescribed for the Sundays of that year. I told him, 'The Commandments'. And I added, 'You're joining the Lord's arithmetic at the right digit. I've got you over the hump. I've just finished with the sixth Commandment.' Then remembering Fr Blake, I continued, 'But you don't have to worry about next Sunday. You won't be preaching on Sunday.'

'No?' he said with the puzzlement of a man who believed that the Medes and Persians had a controlling say in the formulating of Canon Law.

'No, for the simple reason that you won't be saying a public Mass on Sunday. It's traditional here. The old actor holds the stage on the final Sunday; the young actor stays in the wings.'

'I see,' he said, but I knew he wasn't seeing anything except the healthy complexion of the salmon facing him from his plate. He would have to wait seven years, as I had waited seven years, to understand why the priest wouldn't want to say all he had to say to only half of the people to whom he wished to say it.

The final occasion on which I made Fr Blake my guide was when Fr Newman wondered how soon he could leave the island for a day or two without giving offence. 'In a month, perhaps?' he suggested nervously.

'On Monday,' I said firmly. 'There's no sense in the two of us being here, and by Monday your head will be so full of Capaillisms you'll have to tell them to someone or burst. And while you're out, ask your father, who is a builder, isn't he, if there's any cure for a chimney that smokes in a north-west wind. You could be bringing back a month of happiness with you on Wednesday if he has any knack for fixing it.'

I wasn't honest with him. The truth of the matter was I didn't want to have him embarrassingly around when my boat would be leaving on Wednesday morning. I had never mastered the drill of the military goodbye and I had no wish to be the amusing bit of the first chapter in another priest's memoirs.

ON SUNDAY MORNING I celebrated the two Masses and instead of preaching I said goodbye. A liturgist would have called me out of the pulpit for desecration of the word of God, but fortunately liturgists never visited us, they always went on their holidays to monasteries in Belgium and France.

I took the view that it was as a priest the people of the island had welcomed me in the first instance, so it ought to be demonstrably as a priest with my chasuble on me that I should say thanks to them at the end of my stay.

And the saying of a word of thanks was surely a more apposite prologue to the Eucharistic drama – considering that on the very first occasion when it was stage-managed by Christ Himself, His psalm was thanks – than the reading of a circular from some Government department urging the people to go out and vote in strength at the general election.

(Actually, I never read out such a circular at all because I discovered that the T.D. who had practically all the votes of the island in his file and who, election after election, slid into the Dáil along the slouch of a Volunteer hat which he had worn thirty years before, visited the island only once every five years, or, if the Dáil was dissolved after three, then once every three years.)

I'm not going to say I gave a memorable address; I'll only say it had one of the qualities of a good talk, conviction. I meant what I said.

I told them they were the salt of the earth and not in the sense in which their windows were whitened after a winter storm. And even if a little of the salt lost its savour from time to time, that was nothing compared to the abundance of God's seasoning which could be found in every house in the island.

I told them things I couldn't have told them until that final Sunday or the wags in the pub would have construed my remarks as a series of flies dropped into the pool of the church to lure fatter dues out of their pockets. I told them I would miss them as I'd miss their sea, wide as their hearts; and I would miss them as I'd miss their mountain, strong as their faith; and I would miss them as I'd miss their roads, leading to the house of God.

In other dioceses in Ireland such a Sunday Mass good-bye wouldn't be permitted because priests are transferred from one parish to another in between two Sundays, for the very good reason that in the past farewells were too often made the occasion for full wallets. All the same, this system reduces the priest to a kind of religious robot who is switched off in one place on a Tuesday and switched on in another on the following Saturday. In Tirella, in spite of the unworthy capers our custom sometimes gave rise to, we liked to remember that Christ said His goodbyes elaborately, first at the Last Supper when He was about to transfer from life to death, and later on upon the Mount of Olives when He was about to transfer from earth to heaven.

ON MONDAY I WENT west the road for the last time. I did the kind of round the postman did at Christmas but it took me much longer than it took Batt because though my mood was far from jovial they all put the kettles singing. I would need to have been Dr Johnson to have drunk all the tea that was cupped for me.

In Mrs Nally's I took the driver's seat near the fire and steered the conversation away from Wednesday. At Mortimer O'Farrell's I gave the two cats, Dusky and Blacky, their final rubs under the chin and they responded with a more than usually generous slobber of satisfaction.

I looked at my bog, mine no longer, now 'the priest's bog' again. Like a child on holidays I pulled myself up to the window-sill of the school and peered in: it had an orderliness I never knew, the kind of orderliness a bedroom has when a corpse is laid out in it.

At the Tanees I added my *benedicat vos omnipotens Deus* to the blessing that Charlie Martin left them when all his gurnet were caught and he was pulling in the final fathom of his line of life.

I called to Grania's Castle to tell her ghost that the ambassador from Rome had been recalled and to request permission to sail on the next galley. It was what people were saying to me at their gates, in their kitchens or crossing their fields that gave me this notion of a status rise but nature soon brought me down again to my junior curate's peg: final performance and all though I was giving, the gander of Ballyheer hissed me off the stage, the swans on the lake didn't even give me a half-swivel of interest as I cycled past and the wind on Trá Gheal had my footprints filled in at one end of the strand before l had finished walking towards the other.

ON TUESDAY I WENT east the road for the last time. Mrs White was 'frightful sorry' to see me go, she said, and the reason was: 'You'd never know but that the new priest might bring in a car the way Fr Courtney did and set the island in a blaze again.'

My Rosary beads got a lot of rubbing as I went east: at the Abbey cemetery where in the scatter of time tens of thousands of grains had fallen into the ground and died; at the strait between Capaill and Leopard where Johnson the Englishman was drowned; on the strand at Cloonabeg from where Michael O'Toole's boat and Pat Howell's boat put out with the ebb of the tide and never returned with the flow.

I didn't look for Jack Boyce in his house. It was too sunny a day to stay home and be satisfied with a window-picture of it. I found him on Trá Eoghain with the sea in front of him grazing on the shore and darting out its small white tongues like cows, and his cattle behind him grazing on the dunes and darting out their small white tongues like surf.

He wasn't in talking form. Another time the sight of the tourists bathing off Trá Eoghain would have plunged him into history: bathers would have become Dippers and his tongue would have wrenched the togs from them and tossed them rudely into deeper water. But not that day. 'Why so quiet, Jack?' I asked.

'Every time a priest leaves, every man and woman on the island is seven years older,' he answered, 'and besides I haven't heard the cuckoo for five days. Could he be gone so soon?'

I called to Jamesy Prendeville's. It was the baking time of the day with him and he was putting some pieces of turf on the lid of his bastible.

'What I want you to do for me,' he said, when he had coaxed the battalion of red coals into position, 'is to give me a blessing.' But before I had time to say, 'All right, Jamesy, go down on your knees and I'll ...' he continued, 'Not the one out of your head, Father. Have you the little black book with you at all? The one with the gold pages? You have! Good. Read something out of that for me.'

I pulled out my Ritual from my pocket. It opened at one of the shattered places where it was trying to become several books. Page 294. *Benedictio Panis*.

'I have the very blessing you want right here, Jamesy,' I said.

'Which one is that?' he asked.

'The Blessing of Bread,' I said and I went over to the fire. 'Bring the holy water.' Jamesy went into his bedroom and returned with a Hennessy bottle three-quarters full of holy water. He knelt down beside his bastible and I read this lovely blessing – 'O Lord Jesus Christ, bread of angels and living bread of eternal life, please bless this bread as You blessed the five loaves in that deserted country place so that the people who will eat it will get health for their bodies and salvation for their souls, things which You alone can give them, because You live and reign for ever and ever.'

'Amen,' said Jamesy and the fire piously muttered when I sprinkled the holy water on the bastible.

My last visit in the afternoon was to Dan Haughton. Going in the passageway I said to myself, 'What will Dan recite? "Eoin Ruadh O'Neill's Welcome to Rinuccini", I suppose.' Dan was a master of the inappropriate. But I was wrong. As I rose to go, after ten minutes spent in praise of his turf and speculation as to whether there was any bog near Leenog half as good, Dan motioned me to sit again and said , 'There's a bit of a poem I want to recite for you before you go.'

'I'd love to hear it, Dan,' I said. 'What is it called?'

'"The Priest's Farewell to the Island",' he answered.

'I never heard that one,' I said, all surprise. I thought I knew all Dan's repertoire and I never before heard time and title so well matched.

'How could you?' he answered. '"Tis like today's cake, still a making.'

'You're a poet, Dan!' I exclaimed. 'And you never told me.' He had his hands together in front of his stomach and his fingers were trying to hide with shyness.

'"Tisn't all my doing, Father. There's four or five of us at it. We make it up the way we plant a hedge. One fellow puts in a bit here and another fellow puts in a bit there.'

'And where's the bardic school, Dan?' I asked.

'Down in the pub, Father.'

'Long may the inspiration flow!'

'We haven't long left to finish it now, Father. It must be finished for tonight.'

'Why tonight?'

'You'll know tonight,' and he smiled with the satisfaction of half giving away and half keeping a secret. 'Will you listen to the start of it now?'

'I will indeed, Dan. Off you go.' He stood at the fire, one hand pictorially placed on the mantelpiece and the other stretched to his audience of cups and saucers in the dresser. He cleared his throat.

'"The Priest's Farewell to the Island",' he announced and began:

The priest was on the mailboat
And the people on the pier
And he saw their eyes of sorrow
And he said with many a tear,
'I may sail south to the Tropics
And climb in far Tibet
But the happy homes of Capaill
I never will forget'.

I HEARD THOSE LINES again that night in the Hall. There was a kind of a command performance and it was the islanders who did the commanding.

At five minutes to eleven, when I was packing my books in a tea chest which somehow had escaped Aggie's kindling hands, there was a knock at the door and three men came in. They were Paddy Mallon, John McHale and Peter Lenny.

'You might say we are a kind of a deputation,' Paddy began. 'Seven years ago when you came to us we were the first three from the island that you met.'

'In Kathy O'Hally's,' John reminded me.

'So we're coming now on behalf of the whole island to ask you to a bit of a dance in the Hall, as 'tis our last night together,' Peter said, putting the final touches to the communal speech.

It was more than a bit of a dance. It was an American wake of sorts: Leenog or Los Angeles, what was the difference when the only kind of nearness that matters is presence? The idea of an American wake is to strangle sorrow with singing, to make so much noise that the mind won't hear what the heart is saying. We had singing and we had noise.

And dancing. The Stack of Barley got such a shaking you

would think the September equinox was already blowing. The Walls of Jericho had nothing on the Walls of Limerick. And there was no sadness in the world so great that it could sally out into the open when the Siege of Ennis began.

Dan recited the full eight stanzas of 'The Priest's Farewell to the Island'. And not only did he speak it to me but he spoke it for me because in the morning when 'the priest would be on the mailboat and the people on the pier' I couldn't hope to have his wind or his steadiness of voice.

It all ended at half-past three.

WEDNESDAY MORNING MOCKED my heart. The sea was calm. After my breakfast I walked down the passage to the kitchen for the last time. Aggie was sitting down, a thing she never did until the day thought of sitting too.

Not once in the seven years had we so few words. All I said was 'Well, goodbye, Aggie' and Aggie said no word at all. For once 'oooh' failed completely as a synonym. It was one of those partings where the eyes didn't meet to part. As we shook hands Aggie looked at the cold oven and I looked out the window at the red tears on the fuchsia bushes.

I left the house and went into the church. There was nobody there. I looked at the empty seats: that was nothing new. What was strange was to think that I would never see them full again.

I walked down to the quay. There wasn't much of the overgrown grass to be seen on it; trousers and skirts were hiding it. It was like the gathering we used to have when the corpse of someone who had died in a hospital on the mainland was expected home.

I remember what happened on the quay only as a member of a family remembers a mother's or a father's funeral. It comes back to me as a dizziness. I recall being twisted round and round. A man would squeeze me on the elbow and I would turn around to say goodbye to him and while I was shaking his hand another tap would put my shoulder spinning again in the opposite direction.

I wish only the children had come. Children are easy to

135

say goodbye to. You catch their noses as if they were door-knockers or you pull their ears as if they were pieces of material on raggy toys and, in a matter of minutes, going away is a game, a bit of fun. But all the women were there and women do not make partings easy.

In one respect God was good to me. The tide was in full and the *Sapphire* was berthed at the quayside. That meant that once the mailboat got under way the pain of parting would be given a quick anaesthetic of distance. If the tide had been low I would have had to board a rowboat at the beach and sail out to the *Sapphire*'s anchorage and the parting would have been as slow as the strokes of the men on the oars.

Just when I had reached the iron ladder that led down to the deck of the mailboat, Jack Boyce came through the crowd and stopped me from putting my feet on the top step. 'I have a little present for you,' he said, 'and I couldn't give it to you last night. The Hall was too hot entirely. They would have died, the creatures,' and he handed me an old tobacco box with the two wild flowers, rare bee orchids, inside. It was Jack's way of saying goodbye.

I started down the ladder. Once I was half way down I always jumped aboard but I didn't do so that morning because there were men waiting at the bottom to give me five or six helping hands. It was their awkward way of making my going easier.

The next thing that happened was what a provincial newspaper would call an altercation in the stern. Jamesy Prendeville was in it and Miley O'Shea and Paddy Mallon and two or three others.

'Let him be,' I heard Paddy Mallon saying to Miley. Because I was, albeit unwillingly, so much at the centre of the morning's whirl I referred the personal pronoun singular number and masculine gender to myself.

But I was wrong. The wrangle really was about who would take the tiller of the *Sapphire* on her way out the harbour. Jamesy had his hand on it and it would have taken a policeman's truncheon to get him to loosen his grip of it.

Paddy Mallon was a peace-loving man always so he let

Jamesy have his way and he did what a sheep-farmer could have done as well: he contented himself with catching the hawser when it was flung aboard.

'Start her up, Miley,' Jamesy ordered and when the diesel mercifully cracked the encasing silence, 'Half speed ahead,' he shouted, and the *Sapphire* quickly left water between herself and the quay.

The people were on the beach, the women at the water's edge, the men farther back up the shingle, the very positions they would have had if they were in church.

The women fell back as the wash from the mailboat heaved in, a line of seaweed at their toes. And then their arms spoke their special language of goodbye and I waved back at them until there was nothing to wave at except a group of boulders on the beach.

On either side of the *Sapphire* as we sailed out the harbour there was a line of currachs and pookauns from every cove of the island. I thought of Mrs White on the hill above Jamesy's and how she would be aghast at this volume of traffic on the waters. A flotilla wasn't something that floated well in Mrs White's cup of tea!

The *Irish Coast Pilot* says that it is feasible to sail 'extremely close' to the beacon. Paddy Mallon, who didn't suffer from nerves, interpreted this as about thirty feet in a flat sea with no swell. Jamesy rounded it that day with less than the boat's beam between it and us, ten feet at its most startling most. It was his tour de force, the way the Skipper, the way *the* Skipper had of saying goodbye.

The escort left us to seaward of the beacon and my mind fell to thinking of a poem I learned going to school: 'At the back of Patrick Lynch's boat I sat in woeful plight'.

It was a long trip to Killeggan.

A MILE EAST of Killeggan on the hill road to Leenog I stopped my car. I turned off the engine and sat there for an hour. I didn't get out to look back at the island nine miles out in the Atlantic. It had shaped my eyes to its own shape so there was no need to look. And if I did, I would have had

137

to sit in the car for yet another hour before I could show those eyes in my new parish.

When the rear mirror told me I was now suffering from no more than a cold in the head, I restarted the car and headed off for Leenog.

Two quotations hitched the spin with me all the way there. One was from Isaiah and it said 'They give glory to God and declare His praise, the people who live on the islands'. And the second was from Dan Haughton and it said 'The happy homes of Capaill I never will forget'.

More Mercier Bestsellers

MY NEW CURATE

Canon P. A. Sheehan

'It is all my own fault. I was too free with my tongue. I said in a moment of bitterness: 'What can a Bishop do with a parish priest? He's independent of him.' It was not grammatical and it was not respectful. But the bad grammar and the impatience were carried to his Lordship, and he answered: 'What can I do? I can send him a curate who will break his heart in six weeks ...''

My New Curate is one of the most powerful of Canon Sheehan's books. It was acclaimed all over the world as a vivid picture of the relationship between a priest and his flock.

ISLANDERS

Peadar O'Donnell

First published in 1927, this powerful novel depicts the life of a small island community in Donegal. It is a story of epic simplicity, of people who confront in their daily lives, hunger, poverty and death by drowning.

'*Islanders* would be worth reading merely as a description of the lives of the poor on a wild, barren and beautiful coast, on which two bucketfuls of winkles may be a considerable addition to the wealth of the home. It is also a piece of heroic literature, however, and as we read it we positively rejoice in the heroism of the human beings ...'

From the introduction by Robert Lynd

PETER CALVAY – HERMIT

Rayner Torkington

This is a fast-moving and fascinating story set in the Outer Hebrides. It is the story of a young priest in search of holiness and of the hermit who helps him. Though the style is fast-moving and all engrossing, the message is precise, authoritative and profound. The principles of Christian Spirituality are pin-pointed with a ruthless accuracy that challenges the integrity of the reader, and dares him to abandon himself to the only One who can radically make him new.

PETER CALVAY– PROPHET

Rayner Torkington

Every ambitious publisher hopes to produce a best seller – every successful publisher dreams of producing a classic. This book embodies both. It is a brilliant exposition of the inner meaning of prayer and of the profound truths that underlie the spiritual life. Here at last is a voice that speaks with authority and consummate clarity amidst so much confusion, of the only One who makes all things new and of how to receive him.

THE GIFT OF A FRIEND
And Other Verses

Carmel Bracken, RSM

The author says she has to listen to the inner voices of loneliness, fear, anger, frustration before she can hear the quiet voices of hope, love, faith and God. The reflections in this book represent some of those voices.

THE RED-HAIRED WOMAN
and Other Stories

Sigerson Clifford

Each of 'Sigerson Clifford's delicious tales ... in *The Red-Haired Woman and Other Stories* is a quick, often profound glimpse of Irish life, mostly in the countryside. The characters appear, fall into a bit of trouble and get wherever they're going without a lot of palaver. The simple plots glisten with semi-precious gems of language ...'

James F. Clarity, **The New York Times Book Review**

MY VILLAGE – MY WORLD

John M. Feehan

This is a book that never palls or drags. It is boisterous and ribald and I am tempted to say that it is by far the funniest book I have ever read. It is also an accurate and revealing history of rural Ireland half a century ago and more. John M. Feehan writes beautifully throughout. I love this book.

From the Foreword by John B. Keane

My Village – My World is a fascinating account of ordinary people in the countryside. It depicts a way of life that took thousands of years to evolve and mature and was destroyed in a single generation. As John M. Feehan says 'Nobody famous ever came from our village. None of its inhabitants ever achieved great public acclaim ... The people of our village could be described in government statistics as unskilled. That would be a false description. They were all highly skilled, whether in constructing privies or making coffins, digging drains or cutting hedges, droving cattle or tending to stallions ... I do not want to paint a picture of an idyllic village like Goldsmith's phony one. We had our sinners as well as our saints ...'

DURANGO

John B. Keane

*Danny Binge peered into the distance and slowly spelled out
the letters inscribed on the great sign in glaring red capitals:*
   'DURANGO,' he read.
   *'That is our destination,' the Rector informed his friend.
'I'm well known here. These people are my friends and before
the night is over they shall be your friends too.'*

The friends in question are the Carabim girls: Dell, aged
seventy-one and her younger sister, seventy-year-old Lily. Generous, impulsive and warm-hearted, they wine, dine and entert-
ain able-bodied country boys free of charge – they will have
nothing to do with the young men of the town or indeed any
town ...

Durango is an adventure story about life in rural Ireland
during the Second World War. It is a story set in an Ireland that
is fast dying but John B. Keane, with his wonderful skill and
humour, brings it to life, rekindling in the reader memories of a
time never to be quite forgotten ...

IRISH SHORT STORIES

John B. Keane

There are more shades to John B. Keane's humour than there
are colours in the rainbow. Wit, pathos, compassion, shrewd-
ness and a glorious sense of fun and roguery are seen in this
book. This fascinating exploration of the striking yet intangible
Irish characteristics show us Keane's sensitivity and deep
understanding of everyday life in a rural community.

MORE IRISH SHORT STORIES
John B. Keane

In this excellent collection of *More Irish Short Stories* John B. Keane is as entertaining as ever with his humorous insights into the lives of his fellow countrymen. Few will be able to resist a chuckle at the innocence of bachelor Willie Ramley seeking a 'Guaranteed Pure' bride in Ireland; the preoccupations of the corpse dresser Dousie O'Dea who felt that 'her life's work was complete. For one man she had brought the dead to life. For this, in itself, she would be remembered beyond the grave'; at the concern of Timmy Binn and his friends for 'the custom to exhaust every other topic before asking the reason behind any visit': the intriguing birth of Fred Rimble and 'the man who killed the best friend he ever had'.

LETTERS OF A MATCHMAKER
John B. Keane

The letters of a country matchmaker faithfully recorded by John B. Keane, whose knowledge of matchmaking is second to none.

In these letters is revealed the unquenchable, insatiable longing that smoulders unseen under the mute, impassive faces of our bachelor brethren.

LETTERS OF A LOVE-HUNGRY FARMER
John B. Keane

John B. Keane has introduced a new word into the English language – *chastitute*. This is the story of a chastitute, i.e. a man who has never lain with a woman for reasons which are fully disclosed in this book.

LETTERS FROM THE GREAT BLASKET
Eibhlís Ní Shúilleabháin

This selection of *Letters from the Great Blasket*, for the most part written by Eibhlís Ní Shúilleabháin of the island to George Chambers in London, covers a period of over twenty years. Eibhlís married Seán Ó Criomhthain – a son of Tomás Ó Criomhthain, *An tOileanach (The Islandman)*. On her marriage she lived in the same house as the Islandman and nursed him during the last years of his life which are described in the letters. Incidentally, the collection includes what must be a unique specimen of the Islandman's writing in English in the form of a letter expressing his goodwill towards Chambers.

Beginning in 1931 when the island was still a place where one might marry and raise a family (if only for certain exile in America) the letters end in 1951 with the author herself in exile on the mainland and 'the old folk of the island scattering to their graves'. By the time Eibhlís left the Blasket in July 1942 the island school had already closed and the three remaining pupils 'left to run wild with the rabbits'.

The Man from Cape Clear
A Translation by Riobárd P. Breatnach of Conchúr Ó Síocháin's *Seanchas Chléire*

Conchúr Ó Síocháin lived all his days on Cape Clear island, the southern outpost of an old and deep-rooted civilisation. He lived as a farmer and a fisherman and his story vividly portrays life on that island which has Fastnet Rock as its nearest neighbour. He was a gifted storyteller, a craftsman and a discerning folklorist. Here he tells of life on the island drawing on the ancient traditions and the tales handed down from the dim past. There is a sense of humour, precision and a great sense of community on every page.

The Man from Cape Clear discloses aspects of insular life which should delight the inner eye of the world at large and enrich every Irishman's grasp of his heritage.